# THE OFF-ROAD SURVIVAL HANDBOOK

JOHN CARROLL

Key Books

**Photo Credits**

Indian Motorcycle: p. 210

Jaguar Land Rover: pp. 3, 34, 37 (top), 38 (bottom), 40, 41, 42, 48, 49, 50 (bottom), 52, 53, 75, 77, 78, 84, 87, 90, 91, 92, 93 (top), 94, 95, 96, 103, 104, 105, 106, 112, 114, 118, 119, 126, 127, 128, 130, 131, 141 (bottom), 156 (bottom), 162, 168 (top), 175, 189, 197 (bottom), 200 (bottom). 227 (bottom), 243 (bottom)

Jeep: pp. 14 (bottom), 15, 18 (bottom), 20, 21, 24, 27, 28, 29, 163

Media Vehicle Services: pp. 36 (top), 50 (top), 79, 93 (bottom), 95, 107, 109 (bottom), 111

Mercedes Benz: pp. 45 (top), 46

Nissan Motor GB: p. 163

RJ Reynolds: pp. 51, 89, 120, 121, 128

Toyota Motor Manufacturing (UK) Ltd: pp. 54, 55, 56, 57, 86

US Department of Defense: pp. 71, 85 (bottom), 97 (top), 138

Wayne Mitchelson: pp. 11 (top), 23, 26, 113, 156 (top)

All other images belong to the author.

Published by Key Books
An imprint of Key Publishing Ltd
PO Box 100
Stamford
Lincs
PE19 1XQ

www.keypublishing.com



ISBN 978 1 80282 261 8



Off-Road text design: © Anna Bocharova/Dreamstime.com

Mountain and vehicle images: ProVectors/iStock

Front cover design: Myriam Bell Designs

Typeset by SJmagic DESIGN SERVICES, India.

DEFENDER
Y442 DEP
SUPERWINCH
DEFENDER

# CONTENTS

NOT ALL WHO
WANDER
ARE LOST

# INTRODUCTION

When people refer to the 'great outdoors' they are right, it is great – as in big – and it is outside, but it is also great, as in fantastic. My own journeys in the great outdoors started on family camping holidays to Snowdonia, followed by Sea Scout days sailing, kayaking and camping, before an enthusiasm for maps led me to college Geography. This led to staff jobs on 4x4-focused magazines, which in turn led to my Land Rover and Jeep adventures of the past 30 years.

My favourite four adventures of many have been, in chronological order: (1) being a journalist on the 1991 Camel Trophy to Tanzania and Burundi; (2) driving a Jeep Wrangler over northern California's Rubicon Trail from Georgetown to Lake Tahoe; (3) driving an amphibious Land Rover 90 from Fort William to Inverness by way of the Caledonian Canal; (4) driving wartime Jeeps along the desert routes in Egypt that were pioneered by the British Long Range Desert Group during World War Two. This book is a collation of the things I have learned, even though each section could be a book of its own. I hope you enjoy it, whether you read it in the comfort of an armchair or on your own adventures, and I hope it encourages you to go off the beaten track. J. R. R. Tolkien wrote in those epic tales of journeys – *The Hobbit* and *The Lord of the Rings* – that 'the road goes ever on and on', and that 'Not all those who wander are lost.' Both are completely true.

Leave nothing but tracks. Take nothing but photographs.

John Carroll

With the British Team on the 1991 Camel Trophy in Tanzania and Burundi. Here, team members Andy Street (standing) and Tim Dray (driving) prepare to winch through a stretch of the notorious Black Cotton Mud.

On California's famous Rubicon Trail in 2004. The challenging part of the route runs from Wentworth Springs for about 12 miles (19km) via Rubicon Springs to a maintained portion of the trail that leads to Lake Tahoe.

Driving an amphibious Land Rover Ninety across Scotland from Fort William to Inverness in 2006. The Land Rover is seen here motoring along Loch Ness.

Motoring through Egypt's Great Sand Sea in 2012, following routes pioneered by British special forces, the Long Range Desert Group, during the North African campaigns of World War Two.

# 4X4 VEHICLES

4x4 vehicles have been in production for more than 80 years, and for many they are a passport to all kinds of adventures. Since World War Two, there have been countless 4x4s, ranging from the utility and commercial models to luxury Sports Utility Vehicles (SUV) in a variety of sizes. What follows is a selection of those that have become most popular for off-road use and overland travel, illustrated with examples of them in off-road and expedition settings.

## JEEP

After World War Two, Willys-Overland of Toledo, Ohio, believed it was onto a good thing with the Jeep, as it had become apparent that many of the new military vehicles, especially the Jeep, would be invaluable to farmers, foresters and ranchers after the war. The last military Jeep of World War Two rolled off the Toledo assembly line on 20 August 1945, but as early as 1942, Jeeps had been experimented with to assess their suitability for use as farm vehicles.

The production model CJ-2A was introduced in mid-July 1945, approximately one month before the cessation of military Jeep production, and featured a similar four-cylinder, L-head Go-Devil engine and 80in wheelbase as the wartime MB but included a three-speed T-90 transmission, which was considered an improvement. More obvious changes included the provision of a column-mounted gearshift and a bottom-hinged tailgate, facilitating easier loading of the Jeep, and the necessary relocation of the spare wheel to the vehicle's side. Many CJ-2As did not have a rear seat, to allow for maximum load carrying in the rear portion of the vehicle. There were also detail improvements, including larger diameter headlights, made possible by reducing the number of apertures pressed in the grille from nine to seven, the number that remain to this day. The fuel filler cap was relocated from under the driver's seat to the vehicle's side, and the manufacturer's name was pressed into several of the panels.

Through the production run of the CJ-2A, there were numerous sequential changes made, and the range of available colours was widened to include Harvard Red, Michigan Yellow, Normandy Blue and Princeton Black.

Production was increased in 1946, when in excess of 71,000 Jeeps were made. Slightly more than 65,000 were made in 1947, and in 1948, CJ-2A production peaked at just over 74,000. Jeeps were shown in numerous

The Willys MB and Ford GPW were the Jeep used during World War Two by the Allies.

adverts, being used to complete farming tasks, for example, while other advertising of this time gave a hint at Willys-Overland's export ambitions for its new machine; one of its taglines read, 'around the clock, around the year,

The wartime Jeep proved itself to be exemplary off-road in all conditions, from sand to mud and snow. This Jeep is climbing El Akaba Pass, near the Gilf Kebir in Egypt.

The Willys-Overland CJ-2A was the first generation of post-war Jeeps. Manufactured between 1945 and 1949, it was the world's first mass-produced civilian 4x4.

around the world'. Another similar advert read, 'Across America, Around the World, the Jeep does more jobs for more people'. It went on to point out that the CJ-2A 'performs four functions for one investment'. It could be used as a tow truck, mobile power unit, tractor or runabout.

The CJ-3A Jeep went into mass production in 1948, overlapping briefly with end of the CJ-2A production run. It would be built until 1953, although CJ Jeep production dropped to 31,500 in 1949. The most obvious 'at a glance' difference between the CJ-2A and CJ-3A is the latter's one-piece windshield, which has two windscreen wipers and a vent at the bottom (some export models retained a two-piece windscreen). Closer examination, however, reveals a plethora of other changes too, including the slight variations to many of the body dimensions. CJ-3A production continued apace, and production peaked in 1951 when 44,158 were made. In the end, a total of more than 138,000 were made

The improved CJ-3A was introduced by Willys-Overland in 1949, and it remained in production until 1953.

during the production period, and there was a brief overlap with the successor, CJ-3B, which was introduced in late January 1953. It was also around the time that Willys-Overland was acquired by Kaiser, to form Kaiser-Willys, in March 1953, so the last CJ-3As were made under the auspices of the new conglomerate.

The CJ-3B, introduced on 28 January 1953, is often referred to as the 'ugly duckling' of the flat-fender Jeep models and was nicknamed the 'High-hood', because of its taller radiator grille. However, this was just one aspect of fitting a more powerful engine. Until now, all the CJs had been fitted with flathead, or sidevalve, engines, but an F-Head was selected for the CJ-3B introduced in 1953, the same year as Willys-Overland was acquired by Kaiser-Frazer. The part of the resulting corporation charged with Jeep production was Willys Motors Inc. Like the earlier Jeep engines, the new one, known as the 'Hurricane' engine, displaced 134.2cid and had the same dimensions of bore and stroke. The new valve arrangement made it a considerably more powerful Jeep, as the larger valves of the new engine offered 20 per cent more power than the flathead 'Go-Devil' engine. However, the new valve arrangement made the F-head taller than the flathead engine, so the bulkhead, hood and grille were made 3in (76mm) taller to accommodate the engine. This change gave the CJ-3B a unique silhouette, making 'at a glance' identification easy. The grille had to be redesigned but retained the seven pressed slots of the earlier civilian models and gained a Willys logo pressed above them. The bonnet has correspondingly deeper sides with the Willys logo pressed in. The one-piece windscreen idea was carried over from the CJ-3A but was redesigned to suit the taller scuttle. Approximately 155,000 CJ-3Bs were made in the US, in what was the longest production run of any of the flat-fender Jeeps between 1953 to 1965 for the US domestic market.

Another factor ensured that versions of the CJ-3B were produced until the 1990s; it became the model of Jeep that was licence-built around the world, notably, but not exclusively, in France, India, Japan and Spain, simply because it was the model of Jeep in production when many of the licence agreements were drawn up.

A CJ-3A with a towing A-frame, photographed in Colorado, US.

## SECOND GENERATION

The second generation of civilian Jeeps was also spawned from a military model. Development of a new military Jeep had started in 1951, and production commenced in April 1952. Military contracts ordered the production of approximately 82,000 M38A1s, and production ran until 1957. The M38A1 was 6in (152mm) longer than the CJ-3B, bumper to bumper, but had an 81in wheelbase. A civilian version of it, known as the CJ-5, went on sale in October 1954. For reasons that will become evident, it later became known as the 'short-nose' CJ-5 and continued in production until 1971. To complement the 81in wheelbase CJ-5, a 101in variant, the CJ-6, was made available in late 1955 and was aimed at commercial users who would benefit from a 40 per cent greater load-carrying area.

Both the CJ-5 and CJ-6 were completely traditional Jeeps, with a C-section steel channel chassis, leaf springs front and rear, a part-time 4x4 system, a three-speed gearbox and a two-speed transfer box. The axles were solid beam items and brakes were drums all around. The body was

A CJ-3A being used for agricultural work in Vietnam during the 1950s.

The Willys CJ-3B replaced the CJ-3A in 1953 as Willys-Overland was acquired by Kaiser Motors. Kaiser dropped 'Overland' from the Willys brand name. The CJ-3B featured a higher grille and hood to make room for the new and taller 'Hurricane' engine.

steel, albeit redesigned from the previous models to incorporate more curved panels, notable in the hood and front fenders or bonnet and front wings. The grille retained the trademark seven slots. Both short and long wheelbase (SWB, LWB) versions were still aimed at working users of 4x4s, and the Jeeps were basic, if not austere. Willys made bold claims about the new body shape, stating that it was stronger and more durable than the earlier models. The 4x4 market began to expand at this time; Land Rovers were being imported to the US in small numbers – International Harvester premiered the Scout in 1961, Ford introduced the Bronco in 1966 and foreign competition, in the form of the Nissan Patrol and Toyota Land Cruiser, was on the horizon.

Kaiser Jeep was just one division of the massive Kaiser Industries Corporation, and, by the late 1960s, chairman Edgar Kaiser sought to provide funds to invest in other parts of his organisation by selling Kaiser Jeep. This company was seen as desirable because in 1968 it realised net profits of US$15m, but there was little prospect of selling to any of the big

A CJ-3B off-road in the UK. This is the licence-built Indian Mahindra right-hand drive version.

The Willys CJ-5 became the Jeep CJ-5 in 1964. It was a civilian version of the Korean War M38A1 Jeep. It was intended to replace the CJ-3B, but that stayed in production.

US automakers because each offered 4x4s and pick-ups of its own. American Motors Corporation (AMC) was a different matter; it was a smaller concern with no 4x4s or pick-ups of its own, but it was also in profit. A merger deal was brokered that involved AMC gaining ownership of Kaiser Jeep in return for cash and AMC stock, and the deal was signed in December 1969.

## AMERICAN MOTORS CORPORATION

AMC took control of Kaiser Jeep in December 1969, and the new 1970 Jeeps were the product of Kaiser Frazier, having been announced in the autumn of 1969. AMC lost no time in making changes to the CJ-5 and CJ-6 Universal models, adding new decals for the bonnet and a new range of options, including a dealer-installed AM radio, rollbar, swingaway spare wheel carrier and a rear step-bumper. A new model, the Renegade, arrived early in the year with strong colours, wide wheels and a distinct hot rod look. It caught the imagination of Jeep buyers, and thus guaranteed that there would be more such versions of the Jeep. To encourage sales, AMC persuaded many of its car dealers to add the Jeep brand to their line-ups.

AMC worked to refine the Jeep products by reducing noise, vibration and harshness (NVH) and improving ride and handling. AMC fitted its own engines into the CJs in 1972, which also had the benefit of offering more powerful Jeeps; the in-line, six-cylinder, 232cid engine was used in the base model, and another in-line, six-cylinder of 258cid was an option, as was a 304cid V8, the only factory-installed V8 engine to be offered in a short wheelbase CJ. To fit these engines, AMC's engineers lengthened the wheelbase of the CJs sightly, taking the CJ-5 to 84in and the CJ-6 to 104in. The extra length was incorporated into the front wings, and the new CJs became casually referred to as the 'long-nose CJs' to differentiate them from the shorter wheelbase models. New transmissions were soon fitted to complement the new engines, and four-wheel drive was provided by the Dana Model 20 transfer box. The axles used were also Dana components, a Dana 30 front and Dana 44 rear. Production of the CJ5 massively outnumbered that of the CJ6; between the introduction of the long-nose models in 1972 and the next raft of changes in 1976, approximately 160,000 CJ-5s were produced, compared with only 11,000 CJ-6s.

The major news for 1976 was the introduction of a new CJ model, the CJ-7, which was built on a wheelbase of 93.5in. The extra length was intended to

The CJ-5 stayed in production for three decades (1955–83), despite newer models being manufactured.

offer greater passenger comfort by increasing legroom and providing more luggage space, but it also created room for a new automatic transmission, the GM TH-400 with the Quadra-Trac 4x4 system, and facilitated the provision of steel doors in conjunction with a moulded plastic hard-top. The range of engines was the same as that in the CJ-5. These were the overhead valve, the in-line, six-cylinder engine of 258cid (4.2 litre) and the optional overhead valve V8 engine of 304cid (5 litre). Disc brakes became standard rather than optional in 1977.

By April 1979, it had become public knowledge that AMC had been in discussions with Renault, and later in the year, AMC announced that a Canadian AMC car plant at Brampton, Ontario, was being recommissioned as a Jeep manufacturing plant, such was the demand for Jeep vehicles. Profits were up for 1978 – total Jeep sales reached 161,912 – and there had been 37 consecutive months of year-on-year sales increases, partially because of the booming four-wheel-drive market. Overall, the 1970s were

A CJ-5 on a logging trail in San Juan Mountains in southwest Colorado.

a boom time for Jeep; it was still an American icon, and one that was able to rightfully claim in its advertising that 'we wrote the book on four-wheel drive'. Production of the CJ-5 and the CJ-7 would continue in parallel until 1983, when the CJ-5 was dropped. CJ-7 production continued until 1986.

The longer wheelbase didn't hamper off-road prowess, and in 1982 it was the CJ-7 that was chosen as the basis of the 30th Anniversary of the Jeepers Jamboree special edition. Only 2,500 examples of this, now collectable, model were built. This was a tiny percentage of the total number of CJ-7s built, which numbered almost 380,000 in the ten-year production run. The CJ-7 sold well because, in this more refined form, it doubled as a family vehicle for many buyers. Golden Eagle and Golden Hawk were also upgraded trim levels for the CJ-5 and CJ-7 from 1977 to 1980 and 1980 to 1981, respectively. These models were easily identified by their large bonnet decals but also featured various additional Jeep accessories.

Kaiser Jeep was sold to American Motors Corporation (AMC) in 1970, and the AMC-manufactured CJ-5 was powered by an in-line, straight six AMC engine.

The Jeep CJ-7 featured a 10in-longer wheelbase than the CJ-5, and its curved door cutaways were reshaped. It was introduced for the 1976 model year and remained in production for 11 years, eventually being replaced by the YJ Wrangler.

A final blow to CJ-5 sales came when CBS News' consumer-orientated TV programme *60 Minutes* screened an episode in December 1980 that suggested the CJ-5 was inordinately prone to rollover accidents. ABC's *20/20* followed with a similar programme later, and the image of unstable CJs became ingrained in the public's consciousness, which led to litigation from those who had crashed Jeeps and pressure from consumer groups such as Public Citizen. It was a sorry chapter, and one that would raise its head again more than once in connection with other off-road vehicles because of the parameters of the vehicle's design. To be a capable off-road machine, a 4x4 needs good ground clearance, a short wheelbase and so on. The CJ-5 was one of the best off-roaders of its era, and so, almost by definition, handled differently from a normal car and had a higher centre of gravity. The problems began to arise during the boom in sales, when many Jeeps were bought for their styling rather than their off-road abilities and began to be used as transport. Rollovers increased, and, while often factors of inexperience, alcohol, over exuberance and driver error were to blame, the image of unstable Jeeps stuck in the public mind and with it negative perceptions of the beleaguered Jeep brand. After an investigation, the National Highway Transport Safety Association (NHTSA) ruled that the CJ-5 was not inherently unsafe but ruled that warning stickers should be affixed to Jeeps stating that off-pavement vehicles handled differently from other cars. These stickers are still found in numerous makes of 4x4. In many ways, however, the damage was done, and the CJ-5, almost three decades old by this point, was coming to the end of the trail, so its makers dropped it from the line-up and relied on the longer CJ-7 and CJ-8 models to run on to the end of all CJ production in 1986.

The announcement of the cessation of CJ production, in the 40th anniversary year of the civilian Jeep and at a time when imports were eating into American products, was greeted with dismay by many and provoked an outcry, which was in stark contrast to the earlier outcry from consumers' advocates. The CJ was, after all, not just an American icon, it was a direct link to the vehicle that had won the war and was as crucial a part of American heritage as the cowboy. Fortunately, the management at Jeep was aware of this and had no plans to let the 'real' Jeep die.

## JEEP WRANGLER

The next generation of the 'traditional' Jeep was formally announced by AMC on 13 May 1986. The initial model, described as a 1987 model, perhaps owed more to the recently discontinued CJ-7 than the future at that point, but it is the Wrangler that carried the Jeep into the 21st century.

## YJ WRANGLER 1987–96

The YJ Wrangler was produced in the Brampton factory and comprised a steel body mounted on a separate steel chassis with leaf sprung versions of the XJ Cherokee axles front and rear. The choice of engines were an in-line, four-cylinder, EFi 2.5 litre displacement or a re-engineered version of the carburettor 258cid, in-line six-cylinder. The manual transmission variants used a five-speed gearbox and the automatic, six-cylinder models, a three-speed unit. The XJ axles were wider than previous Jeep axles, so plastic

The TJ was introduced in 1997 as a second-generation Wrangler. Significant suspension changes had been made, and all Wranglers were fitted with coil-spring instead of leaf-spring suspension.

wheel arch extension trims were a standard fitment to the CJ-7 rear tub. Crucially though, the front sheet-metal forward of the cowl was all new and now included square headlights and an angled radiator grille. It changed the appearance of the Jeep considerably and was a subject of much discussion. A less obvious but important change between the design of the CJ-7 and the new YJ Wrangler was the suspension, which was altered following some useful market research into changing fashions. It was had been noted that, in 1978, a mere 17 per cent of Jeep buyers used their CJs as everyday transport, but that by 1986, this figure had rocketed to 95 per cent. This change in buyers also led to a decline in the number of owners using their Jeeps off-road frequently, going from 37 per cent to 7 per cent. These trends would have been evident when development began on the new Jeep, so a lower centre of gravity was achieved, which, along with the wider-track axles, was intended to achieve a better on-road ride and handling characteristics. Three levels of trim were offered; base model, Sport Decor and Laredo, and the 'entry level' Wrangler S followed a year later, as did the Sahara, a 'theme concept' model aimed at those with an outdoor lifestyle. The Wrangler went unscathed through the August 1987 acquisition of AMC Jeep by Chrysler, and by 1989, the range of Wrangler variants started with the Wrangler S and progressed through the Base, the Islander, the Sahara and the Laredo. A comprehensive range of extra-cost optional extras, including types of seat fabric, alloy wheels, stereo radio cassettes, hard-tops, tilt columns, automatic transmission and an 'off-road' package, was variously available across this range. This sales technique worked, and Wrangler sales increased month-on-month from September 1987 until the introduction of the 1990 models, which continued with the proven range of Wranglers. For 1993, Wrangler production was transferred from the Brampton plant to Chrysler's Toledo plant.

From the late 1940s onwards, Jeep offered 4x4 pick-ups and station wagons for both commercial and recreational users. This is a 1960s' Gladiator pick-up with a demountable camper.

## TJ WRANGLER 1997–2006

The next generation of the Jeep appeared in 1997, and, despite retaining the same name and similar SE, Sport and Sahara variants, it was a massively re-engineered machine. From the exterior, the new model looked like a subtly redesigned version of the YJ, although the return to round headlights was immediately obvious and widely welcomed. While the engines were carried over from the YJ models, most of the changes were under the skin of the new TJ, most notably the shift to coil-spring suspension back and front, a system referred to as 'Quadra-Coil' by Jeep. The coil-sprung axles offered greater axle articulation off-road, improved handling on-road and gave a higher level of comfort for driver and passengers. The axles featured a five-link control system with upper and lower control arms that controlled fore and aft movement and a Panhard rod that controlled lateral movement. Dana axles, a 30 and a 35, front and rear, respectively, were carried over from the YJ, although the considerably stronger Dana 44 rear was an option for

The JK, the third-generation Wrangler, was released in 2006 for the 2007 model year, and by now Jeep was offering long wheelbase (LWB) versions, known as the JK 'Unlimited', which had four doors. The fourth-generation Wrangler, the JL, was unveiled for the 2018 model year.

The radical 2003 Jeep Wrangler Rubicon, named after the famous California trail, was the most capable vehicle ever produced by the Jeep brand. It featured air-locking differentials in both axles.

off-roaders. Sales of the new model began with the four-cylinder version, but this was quickly followed by the six-cylinder variant. The TJ sold well in the US and in export markets including Great Britain, so few changes were made for 2000, 2001 and 2002.

A new engine appeared in 2003 TJ models; it was a 16-valve, 2.4-litre DOHC in-line four-cylinder that produced 147hp. It offered more performance than the previous four-cylinder engine, but what was more popular with many buyers was the new four-speed automatic overdrive transmission. However, the biggest news for 2003 was the introduction of the Rubicon model TJ. Named after what is, arguably, the world's most famous recreational off-road trail – the Northern California Rubicon trail – the intentions of this Jeep were obvious. As such, it is one of the most capable factory-built 4x4s ever. The Rubicon TJ had Dana 44 axles with air-actuated

The 4x4 Jeep Liberty (KJ) – Jeep Cherokee (KJ) outside North America – is a compact, unibody SUV that was introduced in May 2001 as a replacement for the Cherokee (XJ) and produced by Jeep until 2007.

Fuji Tru-Lok locking differentials front and rear. It featured a low-ratio transfer box known as the Rock-Trac, heavy duty prop shafts and universal joints (UJs) and Goodyear MTR tyres on alloy wheels.

## WRANGLER UNLIMITED

In January 2004, the Wrangler Unlimited was announced as a 2004/05 model. It was a TJ built on a chassis with a 103.4in wheelbase. The extra length was all behind the driver and passenger seats in order to give the TJ more carrying capacity.

The 2007 model saw another complete redesign of the Jeep Wrangler, in both two- and four-door form. The extant TJ platform was replaced by the JK platform, which was available in two versions: the short-wheelbase two-door and the long-wheelbase Unlimited four-door. The new model was significantly larger than the existing one, with a slightly longer wheelbase and a wider track. Despite this, the two-door model was 2.5 inches (64mm) shorter in overall length than the TJ, providing better approach and departure angles for off-road use. The ramp breakover angle was unchanged, despite the longer wheelbase, because larger-diameter tyres were fitted. Jeep maintained the classic seven-bar grille appearance but re-engineered it so that the new model's noted off-road ability did not compromise its on-road handling characteristics.

The new model comprised a new chassis, redesigned exterior and a refreshed interior design, new engines, Electronic Stability Programme (ESP) and brake traction control across the range in both wheelbases. The all-new chassis was 100 per cent stiffer in bending and 50 per cent stiffer in torsion, and this, together with a refined five-link coil suspension front and rear, gave a more refined on-road ride. New steering and suspension geometry provided precise ride and handling characteristics. A 230.5cid (3,778cc) V6 engine producing 205hp (153kW) and 240ft/lb (325Nm) became the base engine, replacing the venerable six-cylinder. The 2.8-litre VM Motori turbodiesel in-line engine used in the Cherokee was offered as an option outside the US, as it did not meet US emission standards for 2007 but satisfied the demand for diesel engines from European markets.

Standard across the Wrangler range was an ESP, which was designed to aid the driver in maintaining the vehicle's directional stability in severe driving manoeuvres on any type of surface. ESP worked in conjunction with the on-road calibrated brake lock differentials, which aim to improve vehicle traction if one wheel is on ice or gravel and the other is on a dry surface. All versions offered an off-road tuned anti-lock braking system and traction control system with an electronic limited slip differential.

# LAND ROVER

## 80-INCH

The Land Rover was conceived by the Rover Motor Company after World War Two. Maurice Wilks, Rover's chief designer, came up with a plan to produce a light agricultural and utility vehicle, of a similar concept to the Willys Jeep recently used in the war, but with an emphasis on agricultural use. Many of the key features of the initial Land Rover design were the result of simplifying the tooling required to make the vehicle and using the minimum amount of rationed materials. As well as the aluminium alloy bodywork and its distinctive flat panels with simple curves, the steel ladder, box-section chassis was assembled from four strips of steel welded at each side to form a box, thus reducing the requirement for jigs.

1948 pre-production Land Rover number 29 is off-road in Wales.

In 1948, production of the Land Rover that would later become known as the Series One, started. In 1950, the headlights were moved from a position behind the radiator grille to one where they protruded through the grille. For the 1952 and 1953 production runs, a larger-capacity petrol engine was installed in the Land Rover, which was proving to be a sales success. The 1,997cc in-line, four-cylinder unit gave the vehicle more power. During 1950, the original semi-permanent 4x4 system was replaced with a conventional part-time 4x4 arrangement that enabled the driver to engage drive to the front axle with a gear lever. Following a year when the headlamps protruded through the radiator grille, the 1952 and 1953 model year Land Rovers used the so-called 'T-grille', named because of its resemblance to an inverted capital T. This radiator grille would endure until the end of Series One production, and a very similar, but differently sized item, would last until part way through the Series IIA production.

Series One Land Rovers have a part-time 4x4 system and a two-speed transfer box and were manufactured between 1948 and 1958.

The 1955–56 Oxford and Cambridge Far Eastern Expedition undertaken by six Oxford and Cambridge university students from London to Singapore used a pair of Land Rover Series One Station Wagons.

## SERIES ONE

In 1954, the first major changes were made to the original Land Rover when its wheelbase was stretched to 86in. The engineering was such that the extra 6in in the wheelbase equated to an additional nine inches in the load bed to provide additional load-carrying ability. The 86in model was offered as a three-seater with a tilt, a blind hard-top van or a truck-cab, and as a three-door seven-seater. This was a variant of the hard-top, based on the same panels but fitted with windows and a tropical roof.

In 1956, the wheelbase of the 86in Land Rover was extended by 2in to 88in in order to accommodate the new 2-litre diesel engine, which offered

The compact dimensions of the 86/88in Series One and its four-wheel-drive system gave it considerable off-road ability.

buyers the choice of engine types. This engine was slightly longer than the 86in chassis permitted, so the extra length was added forward of the bulkhead. The first LWB Land Rover made was the 107in in both pick-up and Station Wagon forms. The LWB Series One pick-up was later offered as a 109in for the same reasons as the 86/88in models.

## 107IN STATION WAGON

The first five-door model of Land Rover based on the 107in was produced from 1956 to 1959 and known as the Station Wagon. It offered seating for up to ten people and was intended to be used both as a commercial vehicle for transporting workers to remote locations, as well as by private users. The Station Wagon came with a basic level of interior trim and equipment, such as interior lights. The Station Wagons were fitted with a 'Tropical Roof', which consisted of a second roof skin fitted on top of the vehicle. This assisted in keeping the interior cool in hot weather and reducing condensation in cold weather. Vents fitted in the roof enabled added ventilation to the interior.

This left-hand drive Series IIA 88in Land Rover disembarking from the Avon raft is acting as a pathfinder vehicle for the British Trans-Americas Expedition of 1971–72.

The Series II/IIA 88in Land Rover was mechanically similar to the Series One, but its dimensions were slightly larger, although this didn't impede its off-road ability. It was made between 1958 and 1971.

All the Series Land Rovers, including the Series III, were suited to the installation of mechanical winches such as this Fairey Winches Ltd unit, which is driven by a mechanical power take-off.

The Series III Land Rover was a slightly revised version of the IIA and featured a few plastic components. It had a production run that lasted between 1971 and 1985.

A loaded 109in Series III Station Wagon in the sand dunes of Erg Chebbi in Morocco. Erg Chebbi is one of Morocco's numerous ergs, which are large seas of dunes formed by wind-blown sand.

The Land Rover was upgraded to coil springs in 1983 (LWB 110)/84 (SWB 90), renamed as the Defender in 1990 and remained in production until 2016, although there were numerous engines fitted during this time.

## SERIES II/IIA

The Series II followed the Series One with a production run that ran from 1958 until 1961. The two wheelbases of the Series II – 88in and 109in – were referred to by the maker as the regular and long model, respectively, but they were generally referred to as the 'SWB' and 'LWB' models. It was the first Land Rover to receive styling design from Rover's styling department. The chief stylist, David Bache, produced the now-familiar 'barrel side' shape on the sides below the galvanised capping on the waistline and redesigned the roof and panel of the truck cab variant, introducing the curved side windows and rounded roof still seen on current Land Rovers. The Series II was the first vehicle to use the now well-known 2,286cc petrol engine, with its nickname of the 'two and a quarter', which became the standard Land Rover unit until the end of Series production, albeit sequentially upgraded and refined. The 109in Series II Station Wagon was introduced with standard 10-seater layout of the 107in Station Wagon but also offered was a 12-seater option.

The Series II and the Series IIA are difficult to tell apart. There were some minor cosmetic changes made, and the new 2,286cc four-cylinder diesel engine could be found under the bonnet of diesel models. Later IIAs are easier to identify, as, from February 1969 for home-market models, the headlamps were moved into the wings on all models and a wire 'cross' grille took the place of the T-grille.

The five-door Series IIA Station Wagon is considered by many as the definitive Land Rover and as the classic Land Rover that features prominently in the non-enthusiasts' perception of the Land Rover, as a result of its many appearances in films and television documentaries throughout the 1960s. At this time, Land Rover dominated many world markets, including Australia and parts of Africa and the Middle East. This model became the preferred transport of many in these developing areas, notably in the hands of aid agencies, explorers, wildlife organisations and oil exploration teams.

LAND ROVER
G4
CHALLENGE
DEFENDER
BT52 CNJ

*Opposite*: Defender 110 models, the LWB versions, were used on the Land Rover Challenge events in both 2003 and 2006.

*Above*: The Land Rover Defender earned a reputation as a particularly capable 4x4 in difficult conditions around the globe. This left-hand drive (LHD) example is pictured in Iceland.

## SERIES III

The Series III of 1971–85 is the most numerous of Series Land Rovers produced, and its production run exceeded 440,000 vehicles. The Series III offered an amalgamation of cosmetic and engineering changes in order to modernise the Land Rover in the face of growing competition from other manufacturers, especially in export markets. The 2,286cc petrol engine had its compression raised to increase power slightly, and this was the first Land Rover to feature synchromesh on all four gears. In keeping with 1970s trends in automotive design, both in safety and use of more advanced materials such as plastics, the simple metal dashboard of earlier models was redesigned to accept a new moulded plastic dash. The instrument cluster, which was previously centrally located, was moved to a binnacle on the driver's side. The traditional metal radiator grille was replaced with a plastic one. LWB Series III Land Rovers had slightly different rear spring arrangements, as well as heavier-duty springs and a heavier-duty 'Salisbury' rear axle to cope with heavier loads. April 1982 saw the introduction of the 'County' spec Station Wagon Land Rovers, available in both 88in and 109in versions. These featured new cloth seats, soundproofing kits, tinted glass, new exterior colours and exterior graphics designed to appeal to the recreational Land Rover owner.

In 2014, Land Rover and the Royal Geographical Society supported a successful expedition to Oymyakon, Russia, known as the 'Pole of Cold', and back. The team travelled more than 35,000km in this Land Rover Defender 110.

## NINETY AND ONE TEN

Production of the coil-sprung LWB Land Rover began in 1983 with the vehicle known as the Land Rover One Ten. Its name reflected the 110in wheelbase and the popular slang moniker of '109' for its predecessor. It's fair to say that the One Ten was, visually, an evolution of the Series III, and it incorporated a one-piece windscreen, full-length bonnet and a revised radiator grille. Moulded rubber wheel arch extensions were required to cover the wider track axles and so hint at other changes. Initially, the engine and some of the body panels carried over from the Series III, but mechanically the One Ten featured considerable modernisation, including coil springs, which offered a more comfortable ride and increased axle articulation, and the permanent four-wheel-drive system as used in the Range Rover, featuring a two-speed transfer gearbox with a lockable centre differential. The One Ten Station Wagon shared many of its mechanical components with the hard-top van and truck-cab pick-up models but was based around a different body that incorporated a five-door design.

The 93in wheelbase version, the Land Rover Ninety, with its modernised interior and taller, one-piece windscreen, took over from the Series III as the transport of farmers and so was offered in basic van and pick-up forms. It was also offered in Station Wagon form to address the growing trend for 4x4s as personal and recreational vehicles. Features included exterior styling graphics and wider colour options, and optional 'lifestyle' accessories. The new coil-spring suspension was crucial to the Ninety's success, as it offered improved off-road ability and load capacity for the traditional commercial user, while the improved ride comfort now made the Land Rover attractive to more of the car-buying public.

## LAND ROVER DEFENDER

Change came to the Land Rover in late 1990, when the model was redesignated as the Land Rover Defender 90 and 110. This came about because it was felt that the original Land Rover needed a specific name too, as the Land Rover badge was on Range Rovers marketed in the US, and the company's new model, the Discovery, was also branded as a Land Rover. Along with the new name came a new turbo-diesel engine based on the existing 2.5 litre turbo unit, but incorporated a modern alloy cylinder head, improved turbocharging, intercooling and direct injection. It was called the 200Tdi and was the beginning a sequence of turbo-diesel engines to be used in Defenders; the 300Tdi came in 1994, the five-cylinder Td5 in 1998 and the TdCI in 2007.

The Defender 110 Station Wagon followed the Defender 90 and 110 models in incorporating the succession of engines under its unique bodywork, but the real news came in June 2000 when a new version was added to the line-up. The aim was to capitalise on a rapidly expanding market segment that was being exploited by the Japanese manufacturers for crew-cab 4x4 pick-ups. Land Rover enhanced the Defender 110 Station Wagon range with the introduction of its 110 Double Cab variant. Complementing already extant Defender pick-ups, the Double Cab featured seating for up to six but also had pick-up load space at the rear.

During the spring of 2007, a major facelift was made to the Defender, in conjunction with a number of mandated emissions and safety-related changes. A major change was the fitment of a new 2.4-litre four-cylinder engine from Ford's Duratorq line and a six-speed gearbox. Legislation from the European Union required the replacement of the four inward-facing rear seats with forward-facing items. In the Defender 90 Station Wagon, the four seats were replaced with two forward facing seats, thus reducing the Defender to a four-seater vehicle.

## MERCEDES BENZ UNIMOG

The Mercedes-Benz Unimog, a multi-purpose all-wheel drive medium truck, was developed as a farm tractor and produce-hauler but with military potential in mind. Production began in 1949. The name Unimog is an acronym for universal-motor-gerät (universal motor equipment). As a result of their off-road capabilities, Unimogs can be

A pair of Mercedes Unimogs on a desert expedition. Various models of Unimog have been manufactured by Mercedes since 1951.

Owing to their off-road capabilities, Unimogs can be found off-road in remote places as expedition campers with bespoke rear bodywork, as seen on this Italian-registered example.

The Mercedes-Benz G-Wagen is a 4x4 manufactured by Steyr-Daimler-Puch in Austria and sold by Mercedes-Benz. It was originally developed as a military 4x4, but civilian models were later added to the range.

In recent years, Mercedes has offered luxury versions of the G-Wagen alongside basic ones aimed at consumers who wanted them as expedition or working vehicles.

found in jungles, mountains and deserts as military vehicles, fire trucks, expedition campers, and can even be seen competing in competitions such as truck trials and the Dakar Rally. The Mercedes G-Wagen is a smaller 4x4 with similar technology.

## RANGE ROVER AND DISCOVERY

In 1967, the Rover Company began its '100in Station Wagon' project with coil springs, permanent four-wheel drive and adequate power. The final design – launched in 1970 with two-door bodywork and a horizontally split tailgate styled largely by the engineering team – featured coil springs, an all-new permanent 4x4 transmission and a detuned 135hp version of the Buick-derived 3,528cc Rover V8 engine. It featured carburettors and was engineered to enable them to function at extreme angles off-road. In its original guise, the Range Rover combined off-road with luxury and offered a top speed over 100mph, a towing capacity of 3.5 tons, seats for five and disc brakes behind all four steel Rostyle wheels. The Range Rover used permanent four-wheel drive, and only one gearbox was available, a four-speed manual unit (with an optional Fairey overdrive after 1977). Like other Land Rover vehicles of its time, much of the Range Rover's bodywork was constructed from aluminium, although the panels were affixed to a steel frame. Apart from minor details, the body design was changed little in the vehicle's first decade. One of the first significant changes to the Range Rover was made in 1981, with the introduction of a four-door bodyshell. Quarter of a century after the introduction of the Range Rover, the second-generation model, generally referred to by its factory code, the P38A, was launched for the 1995 model year as a five-door SUV. It would stay in production until 2001, and power came from an updated version of Rover's venerable V8, although there was an option of a 2.5-litre, in-line, six-cylinder, turbo-diesel BMW unit. The so-called 'third-generation' Range Rover of 2002 moved the prestige SUV model further up-market.

# LAND ROVER DISCOVERY

The Land Rover Discovery was introduced in 1989 and was based on the chassis and LT77 transmission, permanent four-wheel drive and a locking centre differential of the Range Rover. It had a lower retail price than the Range Rover and was aimed at a larger sector of the car market with the intention of competing with the tide of Japanese SUV imports. The Discovery was initially only available as a three-door version, and the five-door variant was introduced in 1990. In 1994, the Discovery was upgraded with new engines, the 2.5-litre 300TDi four-cylinder diesel and 3.9-litre Rover V8. The stronger R380 gearbox was fitted to all manual models and combined with the flexible cardan coupling on the rear propshaft for more comfort. Production ended in 1998, when the Series II Discovery debuted with the new Td5 diesel engine, although V8 models were offered. It followed in the US a year later with only the petrol engines. Land Rover promoted the fact that the vehicle had been given a complete makeover to the extent that, while still similar in appearance to the outgoing Discovery, every body panel had been redesigned.

Powered by a 3.5-litre Rover V8 developing 156bhp, mated to a four-speed manual gearbox and two-speed transfer box, the 1970 Range Rover was designed to 'be driven off a road and across a field at speeds of 40–50mph'.

Land Rover introduced the Discovery 3, or LR3, in the US in April 2004. It had no components in common with the outgoing Discovery 2 model but retained its key styling features, such as the stepped roofline and asymmetric rear window. It is constructed in what Land Rover calls an Integrated Body Frame, which is where the body is a monocoque, mounted on a steel ladder chassis to which are also mounted the gearbox and suspension. It was the first Land Rover offered with a rear-locking differential and full independent suspension. This comprises an air system, which enables the ride-height of the vehicle to be adjusted by inflating or deflating the air bags to enhance off-road or on-road driving, respectively. The engine, intended for volume sales in Europe, was a Peugeot-developed 2.7 litre, 195bhp, TDV6 diesel linked to a six-speed manual transmission – although this is an automatic transmission variant – a two-speed transfer box and permanent four-wheel drive. A computer-controlled locking centre differential maintained traction on difficult terrains. The Discovery 3 incorporated comprehensive electronic systems, including Hill Descent Control, Electronic Traction Control, Dynamic Stability Control and Terrain Response. The latter enables the driver to select a terrain type on a dial on the dash: Sand, Grass, Gravel and Snow, Mud and Ruts and Rock Crawl. It was followed by the Discovery 4 in 2009, which moved the model further upmarket.

The prototype Range Rovers were extensively tested in Morocco during 1969.

One of the pair of LHD Range Rovers used on the British Trans-Americas Expedition of 1971–72 is loaded for rafting across a river by British Army personnel in the roadless, 250-mile Darién Gap on the Isthmus of Panama. The raft comprised Avon inflatable dinghies onto which the Range Rovers were loaded using the expedition's aluminium bridging ladders.

Range Rovers were used on the 2006 G4 Challenge, in which 18 nations participated and the stages of which were held in Thailand, Laos, Brazil and Bolivia.

The internationally renowned Camel Trophy competition relied on the Discovery 1 as team transport from 1990 onwards. This image was taken in Guyana in 1992.

The Discovery I was very similar mechanically to the first generation Range Rover, so was imbued with considerable off-road ability. This Discovery is crossing a gully during the 1993 Camel Trophy in Sabah, Malaysia.

A Discovery Series II in the 2003 G4 Challenge specification. This G4 Challenge competition had 16 participating nations and visited the USA, South Africa and Australia over 28 days.

The re-engineered Discovery 3 was team transport for the 2006 G4 event in Thailand, Laos, Brazil and Bolivia.

The Discovery was updated in 2009 as the Discovery 4. In February 2012, the millionth Discovery was made. To celebrate this, the 'Journey of Discovery', a 50-day, 8,000-mile adventure, saw three Land Rover Discovery 4s travel from Birmingham, England, to Beijing, China.

# TOYOTA LAND CRUISER

The Toyota Land Cruiser has existed for almost 70 years, and more than ten million have been sold, so, wherever you travel in the world, you are likely to encounter the proven 4x4. Land Cruisers have been sold in the USA continuously since 1958, and Toyota sold its ten-millionth Land Cruiser during the summer of 2019 in Australia, the Land Cruiser's largest market.

Land Cruiser heritage stretches back to 1950, and the vehicle was originally developed for military use. Japan's National Police Reserve Forces wanted a rugged, locally built all-terrain four-wheel-drive vehicle, and Toyota demonstrated its BJ model with a 3.4-litre, in-line, six-cylinder engine with plenty of low-speed torque.

In July 1951, Toyota test driver Ichiro Taira drove one up the trail on Japan's 12,388ft Mount Fuji, further up the mountain than any motor vehicle had previously gone. In 1954, Toyota renamed the BJ as the Land Cruiser, and for 1955, Toyota introduced the Land Cruiser 20 Series with a more powerful 3.9-litre engine. It relied on a super-low 5.53:1 first-gear ratio for handling steep inclines. It was still a spartan machine, but it found early markets in South America and the Middle East because many established markets were already well-served by American and European car makers. This prompted the company to focus instead on the emerging markets. Toyota offered several body styles for the 20 Series, including a pick-up truck, station wagon and a chassis-cab.

The Land Cruiser 40 Series FJ40 was introduced in 1960 – including in the US – and was based around a chassis with a beam front. Rear axles on leaf springs continued, but angular styling, a flat white roof, wrap-around rear windows and short overhangs established the 4x4's new look. The FJ40 was the first Land Cruiser with a two-speed transfer case, which improved off-road capability and greatly contributed to the Land Cruiser legend. Toyota developed the Land Cruiser 55 Series wagon model for 1967, on a 16in-longer wheelbase and featuring its own modern styling and an improved engine. Global demand increased to

The Toyota Land Cruiser's heritage stretches back to the utility BJ models of 1950.

the point where Toyota built its 100,000th Land Cruiser in 1968, and the 300,000th in 1973. Both 40 and 55 Series models gained a new 4.2-litre in-line six-cylinder engine in 1975, and a four-speed transmission replaced the three-speed. For 1980, Toyota replaced the Land Cruiser 55 Series with the all-new 60 Series FJ60, which offered greater comfort while still retaining its off-road capability. FJ40 sales ended in the US in 1983, and their manufacture stopped the following year. A new model, the Land Cruiser 70 Series, replaced the FJ40 in many markets, though not in the US. The Land Cruiser models evolved slowly through the 1980s and 1990s, decades that saw significant growth in the SUV market. In 2018, Toyota sold 318,000 Land Cruiser models worldwide (all versions included).

Toyota introduced the Land Cruiser 20 Series 4x4 in 1955, and these became known the world over.

The Land Cruiser FJ40 Series 4x4 was introduced in 1960, powered by an in-line six-cylinder engine.

## TOYOTA 70 SERIES LAND CRUISER

In much of the world, especially Africa and Australia, one particular four-wheeler has a reputation for being as hard as nails and virtually unbreakable even in the harshest environments. The 4x4 in question is Toyota's 70 Series Land Cruiser, a model that has covered millions of miles in Africa's deserts, earning an enviable reputation for its versatility, ruggedness and sheer dependability. Its specification includes a 4,146cc in-line six-cylinder, normally aspirated diesel engine connected to a Toyota five-speed manual gearbox and a two-speed, part-time, manual selection transfer box and beam axles on coil springs. One real hard worker in the range is the LWB hard-top version, known as 'The Troopie'. The basic 70 Series body has been around since 1984 but was upgraded in 2007 with some mild exterior upgrades. Despite that, the 70 Series remains something of an anachronism, paying little regard to current

The 80 Series Land Cruiser was introduced in 1990. Full-time and part-time 4x4 systems were offered in different markets around the world.

vehicle styling conventions. In factory-stock configuration, it will approach obstacles of 35 degrees and has a departure angle of 25 degrees. The mechanical upgrades were to make the 70 Series Land Cruiser even tougher: a wider front track, improved suspension and improved steering. The former improved stability, while a revised stabiliser bar and lateral control rod improved suspension rigidity and durability.

Being built for use in remote places, the 70 Series has no turbocharger to fail and has the drag link hidden behind the axle, out of harm's way, and its suspension arms are huge castings. Because fuel stops may be a long way apart, it has two fuel tanks – each of which holds 24 US gallons of diesel. Finally, because it is for use in deserts, an air filter as big as a bucket keeps the dust at bay. Inside, the Troopie is basic – lots of bare plastic, painted steel, rubber mats and vinyl-covered seats. Anachronistic or not, the Troopie, which is still in production for Africa, Australia and South America, recalls the days when 4x4s were UVs rather than SUVs.

An 80 Series Land Cruiser in Egypt's Western Desert. The Land Cruiser was popular in African countries.

For the 21st century, the J200 Land Cruiser Series was unveiled in 2007, followed by the J300 Series in 2020. Both models still used body-on-frame construction.

The Toyota HZJ75 Land Cruiser is a rugged and reliable utility 4x4, with proven off-road credentials. The 70 Series was introduced in 1984 and is still in production.

# OFF-ROAD DRIVING

## FOUR-WHEEL DRIVE

A four-wheel-drive, 4WD, 4×4 or four-by-four, vehicle is a four-wheeled vehicle with a drivetrain that enables all four wheels to be driven by the engine and transmission. 4×4 originated as a military term; the first '4' is the total number of wheels on the vehicle and the second is the number of driven wheels (the numbers are actually axle-ends, which allow for more

### 4X4 SURVIVAL ESSENTIALS

- Ample supply of drinking water – carry a reserve container
- First aid kit (see 'First aid kit essentials' list on page 231)
- Extra clothes, especially warm outer layers, such as a waterproof jacket and woolly hat
- Emergency blanket or bivvy bag
- Matches and/or a lighter
- Maps of the area you plan to visit and a compass
- Plenty of food – bring more than you think you'll need for the length of your trip
- Recovery equipment (see 'Recovery essentials' list on page 96)
- Shovel
- Spare equipment (see 'Spare essentials' list on page 212)
- Sunscreen
- Vehicle tool kit (see 'Tool kit essentials' list on page 211)

The exceptionally difficult conditions encountered on the 1989 Camel Trophy in the Amazon Basin.

## FOUR-WHEEL-DRIVE SYSTEMS

Most 4WD/AWD (all-wheel drive) systems fall into one of four categories:

- F4: Front-engine, rear-wheel-drive-derived 4WD/AWD layout (e.g., Mitsubishi L200, Ford Ranger).
- R4: Rear-engine/all-wheel-drive system (VW Synchro).
- FF4-T: Front-engine transversely mounted/front-wheel-drive-derived AWD layout (Land Rover Freelander).
- FF4-L: Front-engine longitudinally mounted/front-wheel-drive-derived AWD layout.

than one wheel on each end of an axle, as in the case of 6x6/6x4 trucks etc.). A 4×2 is a four-wheel vehicle in which engine power is transmitted to only two axle-ends: the front two in front-wheel-drive configuration or the rear two in a rear-wheel-drive vehicle.

4x4 is now generally associated with off-road vehicles and SUVs; typically, larger passenger vehicles that may automatically, or enable the driver to manually, switch between two-wheel-drive (2WD) mode for streets and

The full-time 4x4 system has become more widely available since Rover pioneered it in the Range Rover in 1970. That system became a crucial part of the 1983–2016 Defender range of vehicles.

four-wheel-drive mode for low-traction conditions such as mud and snow. However, powering all four wheels can provide better control for normal road cars on many surfaces, as is shown on the Jensen FF, Audi Quattro and Subaru Impreza.

## FULL-TIME 4X4

Because all four wheels in a full-time 4x4 system are connected by a system of three differentials, they would, without centre differential locks, become stuck when any one of the four tyres lost traction. However, unlike a part-time 4x4 system, full-time 4x4 can be used on tarmac without damaging the differentials through 'wind-up' because it employs a centre differential, which enables each axle to rotate at a different speed. Typical lever or switch settings are 4WD High and 4WD Low. A prominent example is the first-generation Land Rover Defender, which is a 4x4 that powers all wheels evenly and continuously via the manually lockable centre differential.

## PART-TIME 4X4

A traditional part-time 4x4 system does not connect the front and rear via a differential, and therefore does not necessarily become stuck if a front wheel loses traction. Part-time 4x4 systems are mechanically simpler and cheaper than full-time systems. The main drawback of part-time 4x4 is that, because it lacks a centre differential, it can only be used in low-traction situations where the wheels have the ability to slip as needed. The part-time 4x4 system was pioneered in the Willys Jeep and the post-war Land Rover.

Selectable four-wheel drive, whether manually or electronically actuated, remains the standard configuration of the 4x4 system in vehicles such as Japanese 4x4 pick-ups. Typical lever or switch settings are 2WD, 4WD High or 4WD Low, and such vehicles are driven in 2WD high range under normal conditions, and 4WD and low range can be engaged as required when ground conditions become difficult.

The world's first mass-produced light 4x4 vehicle, the Willys Jeep featured a part-time 4x4 system that was soon proven off-road in all conditions. Here, Rick Pewe is seen driving such a Jeep on Egyptian sand.

4x4s with locking differentials in their axles and gearboxes are able to climb most obstacles, as this Mercedes G-Wagen shows.

# THE HARDWARE

## Centre differential

When powering two wheels simultaneously, the wheels must be allowed to rotate at different speeds as the vehicle goes around bends. The problem is even more complicated when driving all four wheels. A design that fails to account for this will cause the vehicle to handle poorly on turns, fighting the driver as the tyres slip and skid as a result of the mismatched speeds. A differential enables the engine to drive two gearbox output shafts independently at different speeds. The differential distributes torque evenly, while distributing angular velocity (turning speed) so that the average for the two output shafts is equal to that of the differential ring gear. Each powered axle requires a differential to distribute power between the left and the right sides. When all four wheels are driven, a third differential is used to distribute power between the front and the rear axles.

## Electronic Traction Control

When one wheel spins out of control when lacking traction, the brake is automatically applied to that wheel. By preventing one wheel from spinning freely, power is divided between the non-slipping wheel and the brake for the slipping wheel. This is an effective solution, although it causes additional brake wear. This design is commonly seen on luxury and crossover SUVs.

## Locking differentials

These work by temporarily locking together a differential's output shafts, causing all wheels to turn at the same rate, providing torque in case of slippage. This is generally used for the centre differential, which distributes power between the front and the rear axles, although aftermarket locking axle differentials are used in extreme conditions.

The two most common factory-installed locking differentials use either a computer-controlled multi-plate clutch or viscous coupling unit to join the shafts. In the multi-plate clutch, the vehicle's computer senses slippage and locks the shafts. In viscous coupling differentials, such as those fitted to some Range Rovers, the sheer stress of high shaft speed differences causes a dilatant fluid, in which viscosity increases with the rate of shear strain, during which the differential to become solid, linking the two shafts.

Some vehicles entirely eliminate the centre differential. These vehicles behave as 4x2 vehicles under normal conditions. When the drive wheels begin to slip, one of the locking mechanisms above will join the front and rear axles. Such systems distribute power unevenly under normal conditions and thus do not help prevent the loss of traction, instead only enabling recovery once traction is lost.

## ELECTRONIC 4X4 SYSTEMS

Many manufacturers of so-called 'soft roaders' often use an automatically engaging 'on-demand' system or a continuously operating permanent 4WD system with a torque-sensing differential. The Land Rover Freelander 1, for example, is a front-wheel drive vehicle that engages drive to the rear axle on demand when a loss of traction is detected. The torque is not necessarily split 50/50 between front and rear. Manufacturers have numerous proprietary names for such systems. The Mercedes M Class SUV is full-time AWD, and the Honda CRV has an on-demand system.

## HISTORY

It was not until 'go-anywhere' vehicles were needed for the military that four-wheel drive found its place. The Jeep, originally developed by American Bantam but mass-produced by Willys and Ford, became the best-known four-wheel-drive vehicle in the world during World War Two. Willys (the owner of the Jeep name since 1950) introduced the CJ-2A in 1945 as the first full-production four-wheel-drive passenger vehicle. The Land Rover appeared at the Amsterdam Motor Show in 1948, originally conceived as a stop-gap product for the struggling Rover car company, and despite chronic under-investment succeeded far better than the passenger cars. Land Rover developed a luxury full-time 4x4 in the 1970 Range Rover that was capable of serious off-road use.

## TERMINOLOGY

Although in the strictest sense, the term 'four-wheel drive' refers to the capability that a vehicle may have, it is also used to denote the entire vehicle itself. The term 4×4 was in use to describe North American military four-wheel drive vehicles as early as the 1940s, with the first number indicating the total number of wheels on a vehicle and the second indicating the number of driven wheels. Today, the term 4×4 is common and is generally used when marketing a new or used vehicle and is sometimes applied as badging on a

The Jeep Renegade is a subcompact crossover SUV launched in March 2014. In standard form, it has front-wheel drive, with proprietary four-wheel-drive systems 'Active Drive I' and 'Active Drive Low' paired with Jeep's Selec-Terrain system.

vehicle equipped with four-wheel drive. Many current manufacturers tend to obscure the true nature of their 4WD/AWD systems behind names like 'Active 4WD' and 'Quadra-Drive'.

## KEY MEASUREMENTS

### Approach angle

The steepest incline angle that a vehicle can approach and drive up without encountering front bumper or undercarriage damage. When viewed from the side, this is the angle between the ground and a line running from the front tyre to the lowest-positioned point directly in front of it, which is usually the front bumper.

### Departure angle

In side view, this is the angle between the ground and a line running from a rear tyre to the lowest-positioned component directly behind it, often the rear bumper or trailer hitch but sometimes the fuel tank or spare tyre. Similar to the approach angle, the departure angle indicates a vehicle's ability to drive off a ramp or obstacle without damaging it or becoming stuck at the rear of the vehicle. Approach and departure angles are also referred to as ramp angles.

## Ramp breakover angle

A measure of a vehicle's ability to drive over a sharp ridge or ramp without touching its underside. The 'included' angle measures the angle inside the ramp while the 'excluded' angle measures the combined angles outside the ramp to the horizontal. A short-wheelbase vehicle with a high ground clearance assisted by large tyres will have the optimal (highest) ramp breakover angle.

The approach angle is the maximum angle of a ramp onto which a vehicle can climb or descend without touching its front.

The departure angle is the maximum ramp angle from which the car can descend or ascend without damage. Approach and departure angles are also referred to as ramp angles.

## Axle articulation

Vertical wheel travel and how far an axle can move up and down. Such articulation enables a 4x4 to keep all four tyres in contact with the ground in rough terrain, enabling the vehicle to maintain traction.

Axle articulation is the ability of a 4x4's axle to move vertically relative to the chassis. The greater the articulation, the better the vehicle will be off-road.

## FOUR-WHEEL DRIVE – HIGH RANGE

In a Series Land Rover, four-wheel drive high range is engaged by depressing the lever with the yellow knob and in other systems by moving a gear lever backwards. Generally, this can be done without stopping the vehicle. In a Series Land Rover, two-wheel drive is reselected by stopping the vehicle and pulling back the transfer lever with the red knob until the lever with the yellow knob springs up and returns to the two-wheel drive position, then returning the transfer lever to its original position. In Jeeps and similar, it involves moving the two/four and high/low levers as required, as some have two levers while others rely on a single lever.

## FOUR-WHEEL DRIVE – LOW RANGE

Low range is generally engaged by bringing the vehicle to a complete standstill and then pulling the transfer lever back through the neutral position into low range. This also engages the four-wheel drive. High range is regained by returning the transfer lever to the fully forward position.

## BRAKING

When off-road on loose, muddy, or wet surfaces, keep the application of the brake pedal to an absolute minimum. Braking in these conditions on inclines will almost certainly cause one or more wheels to lock, and the resulting slide can prove dangerous and difficult to control.

## ENGINE BRAKING

Before descending steep inclines, stop the vehicle and engage first gear, low range on vehicles fitted with manual transmissions. While descending the incline, the engine will provide sufficient braking effort to control the vehicle's descent. The brakes should not be applied, as this may cause the wheels to lock on loose or slippery surfaces, resulting in loss of control.

## DRIVING ON SOFT GROUND

When driving in soft ground conditions such as sand or mud, bear in mind that reduced tyre pressures will increase the contact area of the tyres with the ground. This will improve traction by increasing tyre flotation, although tyres can come off the wheel rim if they are too low. Of course, tyre pressures must be returned to normal as soon as possible and definitely before returning to surfaced roads, and foot pumps and plug-in electrical pumps are readily available for this. Refer to the vehicle instruction manual for advice on maximum tyre pressures, and work to 12psi as a rule of thumb for low pressure.

## DRIVING ON ROUGH TRACKS

Although many rough and unsurfaced tracks can be negotiated in two-wheel drive, it is advisable to select four-wheel drive if there is excessive suspension movement, as this may induce wheel spin. On vehicles

A US Army High Mobility Multipurpose Wheeled Vehicle (HMMWV) on a mountain track typical of the terrain in Afghanistan.

The centre differential, where fitted, should be locked before attempting rocky sections rather than waiting until you're wedged on a rock before engaging it.

such as Range Rovers and Land Rovers equipped with permanent four-wheel-drive systems, the centre differential should be locked. If the track or route deteriorates, it may be necessary to engage low range to enable a steady slow speed to be maintained without repeated use of the brake and clutch pedals.

## CLIMBING STEEP SLOPES

When ascending or descending inclines, it is important to follow the fall line, as crossing diagonally may result in the vehicle sliding sidewards or rolling down the incline. When ascending steep inclines, especially where the surface is loose or slippery, it helps to take advantage of a vehicle's momentum. Too much speed when climbing a bumpy surface can result in one or more wheels lifting, causing the vehicle to lose traction and fail the climb. In such a situation, a slower approach may be successful. Traction can often be improved by easing off the accelerator immediately before loss of forward motion.

# FAILED HILL CLIMBS

If the 4x4 fails to climb a hill but does not stall, the following procedure that applies to vehicles fitted with automatic or manual transmission should be adopted:

1. Hold the vehicle on the foot brake. It will be necessary to use the handbrake only if the foot brakes fail to hold as a result of wet brake linings.
2. Engage reverse gear low range as quickly as possible.
3. Release the brakes and clutch simultaneously.
4. Allow the vehicle to reverse down the fall line of the incline, enabling the engine's overrun braking to control the speed of decent.
5. Do not apply the brake pedal during the descent to avoid locking the front wheels and rendering the steering ineffective.

If the engine has stalled, follow this procedure for vehicles fitted with manual transmission:

1. Hold the vehicle on the foot/hand brake.
2. Engage reverse gear low range and remove feet from brake and clutch pedals.
3. Start the engine in gear and allow the vehicle to reverse down the hill using engine overrun braking to control the speed of descent. Remember also that a laden vehicle on a steep hill will start without the aid of the starter motor, as the brakes are released where there is sufficient traction.

If the engine has stalled on a vehicle fitted with an automatic transmission, the brakes should be applied, and the engine must be restarted before reversing downhill, as there will be no braking effort from the gearbox unless the engine is running.

# GROUND CLEARANCE

It is important to ensure ground clearance under the chassis and axle differentials and to use clear approach and departure angles. Avoid deep

Ground clearance is the minimum distance from the ground to the underside of a 4x4, excluding its tyres and wheels.

wheel ruts, sudden changes of slope and obstacles that may catch the chassis or axles. On soft ground, the axle differentials will generally clear their way in all but the most difficult conditions. On frozen, rocky or dry hard ground, contact between the differentials and the ground often result in the vehicle coming to a halt.

## RUTTED TRACKS

Avoid oversteering while driving in ruts, as it can result in the vehicle being driven on full lock along the ruts. This is to be avoided, as it causes drag at the front wheels and can be dangerous when the front wheels reach level ground or find traction, because the vehicle may suddenly veer off the track.

The greater a 4x4's ground clearance, the deeper the ruts it will be able to handle, as this Land Rover Discovery 3 shows.

In V-gullies, drive with the wheels straddling it so you don't end up jammed at an angle.

## V-SHAPED GULLIES

Such obstacles should be tackled with caution, as steering up one side of the gully walls could lead to the vehicle being stuck with one side against the ground.

## CROSSING RIDGES

Where possible, approach a ridge at a right angle so that each axle pair of wheels cross together. If, however, the ridge is a 'knife edge', it may be necessary to approach at an angle until one wheel leaves the ground and the vehicle 'rocks' over the ridge. As it does, the vehicle should then be immediately steered down the fall line. Without axle differential locks, traction can be lost completely when diagonally opposite wheels lift off the ground simultaneously.

When crossing a ditch, enter at an obtuse angle, dropping and removing one wheel at a time into and from the gully to avoid becoming stuck.

## CROSSING A DITCH

Ditches should be treated similarly to ridges and crossed at an angle so that three wheels maintain contact with the ground, assisting the passage of the fourth wheel through and across the ditch. If approached straight-on, the front wheels can drive into the ditch into a position where the vehicle's chassis rests on the lip of the ditch and/or the front bumper becomes stuck on the opposite side of the ditch.

## TRAVERSING A SLOPE

Traversing a slope should be undertaken with care and some precautions:

- Check that the ground is firm under all wheels and that the ground is not slippery.
- Check that the downhill wheels are not likely to drop into any depressions in the ground that will increase the angle of lean.

- Ensure that the uphill wheels will not run over rocks, tree roots or similar obstacles that will increase the angle of lean.
- Any load carried in the vehicle should be evenly distributed as low as possible and secured. A sudden shift of load while traversing a slope can cause the vehicle to overturn. Passengers in the rear should sit on the uphill side.

## DRIVING ON SAND

To cross sand, a low gear and some momentum is required. Lowering tyre pressures to 15psi minimum will create a greater surface area of tyre on the sand, thus spreading the weight. If wheels spin, ease off the throttle and slow down to regain traction. When stopping on sand, halt on a downward slope where possible, as this will help the vehicle pull away on restarting. Sand

It is necessary to have momentum before starting to climb a sand dune. If possible, drive up the axis of the slope.

When stuck in sand, try to reverse out. The tracks you drive in on are often solid enough to drive out on as well, especially when helped with a push.

affects how your vehicle turns. To turn, apply a little throttle as you turn the steering wheel and keep movements smooth. Reinflate tyres on returning to tarmac. Airing down tyres is beneficial on sand but driving at highway speeds on low pressures can cause blowouts or rollovers. To avoid this, carry an electric pump to reinflate tyres.

When driving in soft sand, it can help to use low range as this will enable you to accelerate through suddenly softening conditions and avoid becoming bogged down. Many modern electronic 4x4 systems offer a 'sand and gravel' setting, and this helps considerably in such conditions.

On vehicles with manual transmissions, gear changes should be kept to a minimum, as depressing the clutch increases drag at the driven wheels and can cause the vehicle to stop. Vehicles fitted with three-speed automatic transmissions are best driven in these conditions in low range with the main selector lever in the second gear hold position, as this will eliminate gear changes that impede progress.

Airing down – lowering tyre pressures means the tyres create a larger footprint, enabling the vehicle to 'float' on top of the sand, and it is less likely to get stuck.

When stopping your vehicle in sand, park on level ground, or preferably with the vehicle facing downhill, as it is difficult to restart while facing uphill.

When forward motion is lost and the vehicle stops, clear the sand from around the tyres and ensure that the chassis and axles are not embedded. If the wheels have sunk into the sand, it may be necessary to lift the vehicle using an air bag or high-lift jack, then build up sand under the wheels before attempting to drive it. If this fails, it will be necessary to place sand mats or ladders under the wheels. Use of a high-lift jack in such circumstances requires use of a base that will stop the jack from pushing into the sand.

Carry a shovel to be prepared for getting stuck. Do not spin the tyres, as this only digs the vehicle in further. Try reversing, and if that fails, use the shovel to create small ramps in front or behind the tyres to help the vehicle climb out.

4x4s often get stuck when going over the crest of a dune, and the middle of the 4x4, and its weight, sit on the crest. Such sand dune driving will demonstrate how much clearance a 4x4 has, as it does not need much of a ridge for the vehicle to get hung up on when the ramp breakover angle is exceeded. 4x4s can also get stuck when they go down a dune and their approach and departure angles are insufficient, causing the 4x4 to 'bottom out'.

## SAND MATS

Sand mats/ladders are worth having in all types of terrain but are especially valuable in sand. When bogged down, dig sand out from in front of the tyres, push the mats snugly under the wheels, then use gentle acceleration to drive onto them and out.

## DESERT DRIVING

On stretches of firm sand in a desert, travel in high range gears. Remember that the sand's surface crust will be stronger, and appear dryer, in the cool of the morning. In sandstorm conditions, turn the rear of the vehicle to face the wind or sheet the radiator grille, turn the engine off and sit the storm out.

## SAND DUNES

Conquering sand dunes is a skill, and there are some golden rules. Avoid bogging by lowering tyre pressures to 16–18psi. Use a tyre pressure gauge to measure tyre pressure and be careful not to go too low, as it risks tyres coming off the rims. In such soft conditions, reducing tyre pressures will help as doing this increases the area of contact with the ground. If the tyre pressures are reduced for soft conditions, they must be re-inflated upon returning to firmer going.

When ascending, it is important to keep momentum up and only stop when it is safe to do so. A run up at a steep dune helps build momentum. Not stopping on inclines and stopping on declines are important. The crucial rule for dune driving is to always go straight up and straight down. Unstable sand coupled with a heavy 4x4 will lead to turns on a dune becoming rollovers. In a failed climb halfway to the top, do not try to turn around but reverse straight backwards.

The key to descending sand dunes safely is to ease over the edge and let gravity do the work. Do not brake and keep the vehicle pointing directly down the face of the dune.

When cresting a dune, there is often a blind spot and drivers can't always see what's ahead. If other vehicles are present, avoid collisions by fitting a brightly coloured sand flag to your 4x4. Most stock 4x4s are capable of tackling sand dunes with minimal issues, as long as these rules are followed.

### DRIVING ON BEACHES

Between the high tide mark and 4m from the sea, sand is usually firm enough to take a 4x4. However, this cannot be taken for granted, so check before venturing near the water. Be aware of areas of mud and of incoming tides.

## DRIVING IN SNOW

In snow and icy conditions, drive in a similar way to driving on mud or wet grass. Use the highest practical gear possible in four-wheel drive and drive using minimal throttle, this limits the amount of torque and will help to prevent wheelspin. Using first gear provides maximum control when descending hills.

# SNOW CHAINS

Snow chains can be fitted to most cars, 4x4s, SUVs and trucks, and they are designed to improve traction on snow and ice. They are a legal requirement in some places, such as Europe, for example, if you are driving to a ski resort in winter. It is important to check the legal requirements, as snow chains can cause damage to road surfaces, and there may be minimum snow coverage limits.

Snow chains are generally sold in pairs and fitted to the drive wheels, although two pairs will often be fitted on 4x4s. When fitting, try to fit them in a safe place away from the carriageway and where possible on a level surface. Fit them by placing the snow chains in front of the wheels and driving onto them. Make sure the fastening mechanisms are on the outside of the wheel for easy access. Next, connect the hooks and tighten up the chains. After driving a few yards, they will need tightening again but are then ready for extended use.

## SNOW CHAIN TIPS

- Practice fitting them ahead of your journey.
- Drive smoothly and slowly (max 30mph).
- Adjust chains as required.
- Check for damage regularly.
- Clean and dry chains after use.

## WINTER DRIVING TIPS

1. Clear ice and snow from all windows and lights, as well as the bonnet and roof, before driving.
2. Use all controls including steering, brakes and throttle gently to help prevent loss of traction and control.
3. Leave extra distance between your vehicle and the vehicle in front of you, as it takes longer to stop in adverse conditions.
4. If planning a long journey or venturing off-road, ensure you have plenty of warm clothing, food and water in case of emergency, and that you have enough fuel to complete your journey.
5. Before setting out on a journey in bad conditions, make the following checks: anti-freeze, wipers and windscreen washer fluid, lights, hazard lights, defroster, oil level, tyres and tyre pressure. Softer tyres increase the area of contact with the ground, and this helps in snow but reinflate the tyres before use on surfaced roads that have been cleared, or where snow has melted.
6. More extreme snow driving may require snow chains or studded winter tyres.

A 4×4 system can be a considerable help in snowy and icy conditions, but it does not help when braking, so keep speed slow and steady.

Modern 4x4s, such as this Discovery 4, offer various electronically controlled drivetrain systems designed to optimise driving in snowy conditions.

Snow chains wrap around the wheels and tyres and are secured to prevent slippage. They enable the tyres to get a grip on snow- and ice-covered roads and tracks.

The Commonwealth Trans-Antarctic Expedition of 1955–58 was a Commonwealth-sponsored expedition that successfully completed the first motorised crossing of Antarctica, via the South Pole. It was led by British explorer Vivian Fuchs and New Zealander Sir Edmund Hillary. The expedition used sled dogs, Ferguson tractors with track conversions, Studebaker Weasels and four Tucker Sno-Cats.

During 2010, four modified Toyota Hilux 4x4 pick-ups transported expedition members of the Indian National Centre for Antarctic and Ocean Research (NCAOR), who were studying snow chemistry and glacial landscapes, on a 4,600km round trip from Novo Air Base, at Schirmacher Oasis, Queen Maud Land, to the South Pole, and back.

In 2007, the BBC's *Top Gear* presenters announced their intention to travel from Resolute, Nunavut, to the 1996 location of the magnetic north pole (rather than its position in 2007) in a Toyota Hilux modified by Reykjavik-based Arctic Trucks. In 2010, similar trucks were driven to Iceland's Eyjafallajökull volcano, just hours before its eruption brought chaos to the world's airlines, for scientists to set up monitoring equipment before the volcano sent a vast cloud of ash 30,000ft into the sky.

# WATER CROSSINGS

Water crossings provide challenging 4x4 driving, and the following information is equally valid for driving through flood or rain-swollen fords.

## WADING

Generally speaking, 4x4s are neither amphibious nor waterproof, and the actual depth that can be traversed varies from vehicle to vehicle. For example, a Land Rover 4x4 can manage submersion of between 50cm and 90cm, so it is necessary refer to the manual to find a vehicle's maximum wading depth.

Check the maximum fording depth of your vehicle. If the depth of water to be crossed exceeds 50cm, consider temporarily removing the fan belt to eliminate the cooling fan spraying water over the ignition system and air cleaner. A sheet of plastic or other water-resistant material fastened in front of the radiator grille to prevent any water from passing through will reduce the risk of saturation of the ignition system.

The wading depth is the maximum limit for a 4x4, such as this Freelander 2, to safely drive through water. It is determined by the manufacturer and takes account of crucial factors such as the location of sensitive electronics and the air intake.

## WATER CROSSING TIPS

1. Stagnant water is often more likely to be a hazard than a river or stream, as flowing water tends to prevent a build-up of silt. Silt in slow-moving water can be several feet deep, so ensure that the river or pool bed is firm enough to support the weight of the vehicle and provide traction.
2. Ensure that the engine air intake is kept clear of the water.
3. A low gear is desirable, and minimal throttle should be maintained to avoid stalling the engine if the exhaust is under water.
4. Slow steady progress should be maintained to create a small bow wave.
5. After wading, if needs be, refit the fan belt and remove any covering material from the front of the radiator grille. Make sure that the brakes are dried out as soon as possible so that they are effective when needed. This can be achieved by driving for a short distance with the brakes applied. If the water was muddy, it is possible that the radiator may be blocked with mud and leaves, and this should be cleaned to reduce the risk of overheating.
6. If deep water is regularly crossed, check all transmission oils for signs of water contamination regularly. Emulsified oil can be easily recognised by its milky appearance.

Being prepared is the key. Put recovery straps and shackles where they can be immediately reached to save searching for them in the middle of a river. A recovery strap attached to the end of the 4x4 is sensible, so that another 4x4 can pull the one in the water backwards or forwards as required. Water crossings are not to be taken lightly, as a mistake could do expensive damage to the vehicle – especially the engine if water gets into its air intake.

At unfamiliar water crossings, it may be a good idea to walk the route first before driving through. Consider whether the water is flowing too quickly to safely walk across. Too strong a current is likely to push a 4x4 downstream, causing it to possibly miss the exit point and so be unable to get out of the water. Allowing the vehicle to cool down before driving in water will help reduce water ingress through axles seals and breathers, and, if you are crossing water frequently, think about fitting extended axle breathers. Consider the engine air intake's height and position and do not let it become submerged, especially if a bow wave builds up in front of the 4x4 during a water crossing. Snorkels are designed to raise the air intake out of harm's way.

Events such as the Camel Trophy saw vehicles crossing deep water, meaning that the vehicles' snorkels were essential. The bubbling exhaust indicates this vehicle was still running.

Taping a sheet of plastic sheet across the radiator grille will reduce the amount water entering the engine bay, providing forward momentum is maintained. Even a plastic fertiliser sack can be used in an emergency. Removing the fan belt temporarily will result in less water being caught by the radiator fan and sprayed over the ignition system and electrical components. Consider securing a viscous fan to something solid under the bonnet for the crossing, to stop it from starting up and getting damaged during the crossing.

Water in the ignition system usually results in misfires and can stall the engine midway across the water. To minimise problems, spray the ignition system with WD-40 or similar before driving into the water. Owners of older vehicles with a distributor cap can seal this with a smear of waterproof grease around the cap's rim to prevent any water ingress. Watch for condensation in the distributor cap, which is caused when a hot engine meets cold water, as this can also cause misfires. Some people waterproof the distributor with a rubber glove over the distributor, with the spark plug and king

In water crossings, maintain a steady speed and build up a small bow wave, as this leaves a trough behind it, which lowers the water level in the engine compartment.

leads protruding from small holes in each of the fingers. The electronics in modern 4x4 vehicles do not like water, so do not exceed the wading depth. On vehicles with electric windows, have the driver and passenger windows fully down. It could become the only safe escape point if you start getting swept downstream. Diesel engines are more suited to water crossings, as there is no ignition system to consider.

Enter the water slowly in low range second gear, and as the 4x4 moves forwards it will push the water in front in a bow wave. As you continue forwards pushing the bow wave, maintain this and keep water out of the engine bay. In the aftermath of such wading on a trip in both petrol and diesel vehicles, check the axle, gearbox and engine oils for any signs of water ingress. Milky, emulsified oil suggests the presence of water so should be changed. Because oil floats on water, in an emergency, it is possible to drain the water from under the oil through the drain plugs, which must be closed as soon as oil appears.

When crossing moving water, where possible, angle the 4x4 downstream so the current will assist rather than hinder. Going upstream increases resistance and builds the wave pushing against the front of the vehicle.

## DRIVING IN WATER CHECKLIST

- Plan a route across.
- Walk the crossing to check depth.
- Look for submerged objects such as rocks and logs.
- Do not cross fast-flowing water.
- If it is too dangerous to walk, seriously reconsider your need to make the crossing.
- Spray WD-40 on distributor and ignition wires.
- Fasten a plastic sheet across the front of the 4x4.
- Disconnect the fan belt if a viscous coupling fan is not fitted.
- Have recovery gear ready for use and connect a tow strap to either end.
- Take off seat belts to facilitate escape in an emergency.
- Use low range second gear.
- Remember that airing down tyres increases grip, especially in riverine mud.

## CROSSING TIDAL CREEKS

Tidal run-out creeks may seem shallow and easy to cross but are often deceptive. Water can be moving quickly, and there maybe deep holes from swirling currents concealed in the base. Walk across them first, check out any suspicious areas and be aware of incoming tides.

## SEMI-PERMANENT CROSSINGS

In the 1960s, the British Army experimented with a novel way of crossing rivers in the absence of bridges or boats. In one training exercise, a Series One Land Rover ran along a pair of suspended taut steel wires for a distance of 110ft. To do this, the Land Rover was fitted with special outer wheels. It was part of an exercise staged by the British Army following techniques devised by the Royal Australian Electrical and Mechanical Engineers (RAEME) for crossing rivers where bridges had been destroyed.

Sapper Charles Grayson of the British Army checks his position as he drives a Land Rover over two suspended steel wires at Fort Tregantle, England.

Members of the 1955–56 Oxford and Cambridge Far Eastern Expedition guide one of their 1956 Land Rover Series One Station Wagons across a log bridge en route from London to Singapore.

Log bridges strong enough to carry the weight of a 4x4 can be made from two pairs of tree trunks roped together and laid across a gully.

*Above*: The route taken by the British Trans-Americas Expedition of 1971–72 was along the 18,000-mile Pan-American Highway. This included crossing the Darién Gap, 250 miles of trackless rainforest where fallen trees had to be crossed with the aid of bridging ladders.

*Right*: As can be seen from the length of these tree trunks, substantial bridges can be built across ravines with two pairs of logs.

*Opposite*: When all else fails, boats can be lashed together to make a platform on which 4x4s can be floated across rivers, as is happening with this Range Rover in Laos.

# RECOVERY AND WINCHING

## TOWING

Towing is the most basic kind of recovery, and a towrope or strap is the minimum amount off-road equipment that should be carried at all times. A tow strap should be rated at double the weight of your vehicle. Ensure you have strong recovery points and load-rated bow shackles to connect the strap to the recovery points.

### RECOVERY ESSENTIALS

- D-shackles
- High-lift or exhaust jack
- Shovel
- Snatch pulley block
- Strops for towing, winching and protecting trees

The conditions experienced by the British Trans-Americas Expedition in the Darién Gap in 1971 meant that the Range Rovers' capstan winches were almost continually being deployed.

The rear winch on a US Army HMMWV is being deployed in Iraq. Such winches can be used to recover the vehicles or remove obstacles.

An eye splice is the traditional way of creating a permanent loop in the end of a tow rope.

The Hi-Lift jack is a popular tool for off-roaders but is only suited to lifting vehicles with steel bumpers. It can also be used as a makeshift winch with shackles and straps.

## TOW ROPES

It is recorded that rope was used in China in the ninth century and that the ancient Egyptians made it from papyrus and palm fibres, but the exact origins are unknown. Modern ropes are made from either vegetable fibre, man-made fibres or metallic wires (such as that used for winch cables). The formation of all rope depends on 'twist'. Fibre is twisted into yarns that are then twisted into strands. These are then laid up or twisted up to form the complete rope. Friction, alongside the inclination of each strand to unlay, holds the other in place. The yarns are composed of threads of fibre evenly spun into yarns. The yarns are formed into strands, and three strands are laid up to form a rope (three-strand rope is the most commonly used). Hawser-laid rope is the most common form of lay; it is an ordinary three-strand rope laid up right-handedly and is a widely used and versatile product.

## MANILA ROPE

Abaca is the proper name for the fibre that is usually referred to as Manila, but it is more commonly known by the name of the port in the Philippines from where it was exported, and where it grows almost exclusively. Being strong and durable, it makes excellent rope. It does not rot, but it does swell when wet and stretches 20 to 30 per cent. Production has declined in recent years, as it has been superseded by man-made ropes.

## HEMP ROPE

Once used almost exclusively in the manufacture of rope, hemp was superseded by Manila, the result was that hemp was used for smaller rope lines. It does not swell when wet so made good running rigging. Coir rope is made from a fibre that is not as durable as hemp. It came from the coconut palm and rots quickly when stowed away wet.

## NYLON ROPE

Nylon rope is the strongest of all ropes in common use. Its properties mean that it is flexible but has excellent resistance to ultraviolet deterioration from sunlight, mildew and rot, and so it is ideal for outdoor use in any weather.

## ROPE EYE SPLICE

1. Unlay enough rope to make about three tucks (one turn for each tuck to be made) and form an eye with the ends on top. That is, the three ends must be running diagonally across the rope from left to right, on top.
2. Take the middle end and tuck it underneath the nearest strands of the standing part, towards the left.
3. Pick up the next end of the left, pass it over the strands with the middle end under it, and tuck underneath the next one to the left.
4. The third end is the most awkward. It has to be led over to the right across the third strand and tucked underneath it from right to left. If all this has been done correctly, there should be an end coming out between each of the strands. Should two ends come out between the same strands, the splice is wrong.
5. For the next round of tucks, each end is led over one strand and under the next, towards the left.
6. As a general rule, two full rounds of tucks are considered sufficient for ordinary purposes and three when the rope has to bear any strain. For neatness, splices may be tapered by adding an extra round of tucks with halved strands. These should be cut on the underneath side so that the short or cut ends are hidden.

It is used for absorbing shock loads, such as when lifting or towing, because of its elasticity and subsequent ability to return to its original length after being stretched. It has good abrasion resistance and can last several times longer than natural fibres. It is also resistant to oil, petrol and most chemicals, so is most commonly used for towing and winching securely, as well as for items such as industrial slings.

## RECOVERY STRAPS

For towing recovery, straps have, in many cases, superseded ropes. The snatch, or recovery, strap has now been the go-to recovery device for 4x4 drivers for some years, and, so long as you have another vehicle on hand, a snatch strap is usually the easiest and fastest way to recover a stuck vehicle. Having the right recovery straps and knowing how to use them can make the difference between pulling your 4x4 out safely or not. A high-quality strap with loops rather than attached hooks is the best strap to use for safe recoveries. Recovery straps are flat with sewn end loops made of nylon. They stretch and are safer, easier to use, nowhere as heavy as chains and available in a variety of lengths. Straps can be hooked over a towball hitch; wrap the strap around a hitch but take care not to bend the pin in receiver hitches. Using a tow, hook or D-ring shackle adapter for a receiver hitch is a better idea. Do not attach a recovery strap to a vehicle's bumpers, axles, suspension or steering rods. The attachment points must be to a secure place on the vehicle's chassis and do not position them so that the strap might be accidentally cut. In situations where the strap may break, lay a tarp or even jackets on top of the recovery strap. If the strap breaks, the lain items will slow the strap down before it hits someone.

# SHOVEL

The shovel has been an essential part of off-road driving equipment gear as long as there has been off-road driving. It is often the first tool that the driver of a stuck 4x4 reaches for. Ideal for unsticking 4x4s in sand, mud or snow, it is better to have something larger than the ubiquitous folding military entrenching tool but not as large as a building site shovel. There are many variations of the 'Jeep shovel' carried on the outside of military Jeeps, and these are referred to as the 'bulldog shovel' in the UK. These were initially used by the British during World War One to dig trenches and are still issued by the British military today.

## HIGH-LIFT JACKS

The Hi-Lift jack, which predates the automobile, was originally a product of the Bloomfield Manufacturing Company, established in 1895. Its predecessor was invented in 1905 and sold as the Automatic Combination Tool, commonly known as the 'handyman', 'sheepherder's jack', 'railroad jack' or 'kanga-jack'. Much later, it became known as the 'high-lift jack' (Hi-Lift is a brand name). The jack's versatility stems from its use for such applications as lifting, winching, clamping, pulling and pushing, so this, along with the long travel it offers and its portability, makes the high-lift jack popular with off-road drivers. It is a tall, manual mechanical jack that uses a ratchet system to lift a vehicle. Moving the handle up and down either raises or lowers a sliding mechanism along a central I-beam. The I-beam is punched with holes that act as a kind of ladder for a pin in the mechanism. A curved lever on the mechanism enables lift or lower to be selected, and after every stroke the pin locks into place to secure the load. The length of the I-beam means that it can be used to lift vehicles higher than normal tyre-changing jacks and for getting stuck 4x4s unstuck. High-lift jacks used to be an essential piece of gear for 4×4s used off-road but are less popular with modern 4x4s, where shaped or plastic bumpers often preclude their use. However, many off-road vehicles have designated lift points, and steel bumpers are a good lifting point.

High-lift jacks have to be used with care, as improper use can be dangerous. To lift, pull down, but keep your upper body and head away from the gap formed between the handle and the beam at all times. Keep fingers away from the mechanism and don't put a hand on the beam while lifting or lowering. With each stroke, the vehicle will raise one notch, allowing it to be lifted, for example, out of ruts. In this example, pushing the 4x4 sideways off the jack should mean that its wheels then straddle the ruts, but such operation must be taken with great care so be sure the area around the vehicle is clear of people and anything else that might get in your way. The Hi-Lift can also be used as a winch if connected to a vehicle and an anchor point and can be used for more conventional tyre-changing duties.

## RECOVERY SHACKLES

Recovery shackles connect your recovery straps, tree protector straps, vehicles, snatch blocks and winches. Traditional shackles are shaped like horseshoes with a threaded pin that locks them shut. Recently, recovery shackles made from strong synthetic rope have also become popular.

## SNATCH BLOCKS

Sometimes, when using a winch, you need to pass your cable through a pulley called a snatch block. Snatch blocks can help you exert more force while pulling and can help when you need to pull around a corner because the stuck vehicle and the rescuing vehicle can't be lined up directly.

## GLOVES

When working with recovery straps, winches and winch cables, wear tough leather work gloves to protect your hands.

## WINCHING

Winching, defined as 'hoisting or hauling with a winch', is a vital technique when using 4x4s off the beaten track because it can help when a vehicle is badly stuck, help a vehicle ascend or descend inclines that are too steep to drive up or down and for clearing obstacles such as fallen trees.

It is a largely straightforward process, although it does require a thorough awareness of the potential dangers and of the limitations of the equipment.

This Land Rover Discovery 90 is fitted with a bespoke winch bumper that contains an electric drum winch made by Superwinch. The fairlead is incorporated into the bumper and secure recovery points are bolted to it.

BC03 OMZ

*Above and opposite*: A winch recovery of a Land Rover Defender is underway on a side slope in difficult terrain.

The consequences of a winch cable snapping can be disastrous. To this end, the user should be aware of the capabilities of the winch and equipment to hand and have knowledge of how to use them safely.

## TYPES OF WINCH

In recent years, electric winches have become the norm for Land Rovers, but hydraulic and mechanical winches were widely fitted in years previous. Of the latter, there have been capstan and drum winches, and both rely on a mechanical connection to the engine and transmission to turn. Capstan winches are generally connected to the starter dog on the engine, while mechanical drum winches use a power take-off (PTO) fitted to the gearbox.

### CAPSTAN WINCH

For many years, a Fairey capstan winch could be ordered as a factory option on Land Rover vehicles. A capstan winch is operated differently from horizontal drum electric, hydraulic and PTO winches. It is powered through gears turned by a propshaft connected directly to the vehicle's

*Above*: Members of the 1971–72 British-Trans Americas Expedition team practising the use of the capstan winch on one of the expedition's Range Rover vehicles at Land Rover's Solihull factory.

*Opposite above*: The capstan winch on this Austin Gipsy 4x4 is being used to pull a pile of three substantial logs during forestry operations. Using the rope looped around the logs, as done here, may cause damage to the rope. To avoid this, a choker chain can be used around the logs and attached to the hook on the winch rope.

*Opposite below*: The use of a pulley block enables the direction of pull from a winch to be changed for hoisting loads, as this Austin Gipsy is doing here with its winch rope running through a single hook block.

engine crankshaft via a splined shaft. Unlike drum winches, the rope is not stored on the capstan and they do not use wire rope. Instead, a separate coil of rope such as ¾in manila with a hook on one end can be used. The hook is attached to the anchor point and the rope turned around the vertical capstan. The friction of the turns helps prevent the line from slipping, and once the winch is engaged it pulls the vehicle towards the anchor point and the rope spools off the capstan.

## PTO WINCH

The popular PTO-driven Ramsey mechanical winch was made in Tulsa, Oklahoma. In 1944, brothers Claude and Rayburn Ramsey founded Ramsey Brothers Tool & Die in Tulsa to manufacture parts, tools, and dyes for the Douglas Aircraft Company. In 1945, Claude Ramsey designed a front-mounted vehicle winch for the recovery of other vehicles from mud and snow. It was a successful unit, and demand for Ramsey Winches grew, so much so that in 1947, the Ramseys renamed the company Ramsey Brothers Winch Company. In 1950, Claude Ramsey purchased his brother's interest in the company and renamed it Ramsey Winch Manufacturing Company.

Also in Tulsa was Braden Winch and Steel, founded in 1924, while Koenig Iron Works was in Houston, Texas. The latter was founded in 1911 in order to manufacture equipment for Texas' oil industry. Among Koenig's products was a winch originally designed for use on oil derricks but of a size that made it suitable for use in other applications. By the 1950s and 1960s, during the initial US boom in the sales of light 4x4s and backcountry exploration, it became common to fit Jeeps, Land Rovers and other 4x4s with a mechanical winch of some sort. The Koenig unit, with a drum that spooled on steel cable, was of the right size to fit between the chassis legs of the popular light 4x4s of the time, and as a result it was among the first winches fitted to vehicles in North America and would remain in production into the late 1960s, when electric winches began to increase in popularity. The Trans-Darién Expedition of 1960, which saw a Jeep pick-up and a Series II Land Rover cross the hitherto impassable and hostile jungle and swamp of Darién in Panama, also relied on Koenig's winch. Both these applications were predated by the

The Ramsey mechanical PTO drum winch – note the manufacturer's name in the end casting – installed on the front of a Land Rover in a steel frame that also carries the roller fairlead.

LAND ROVER
MODEL LR-592 FRONT OR CAB CONTROLLED
KING WINCH KOENIG IRON WORKS, INC. HOUSTON, TEXAS


The Koenig King LR-592 winch was a PTO-type winch that was a popular fitment for Land Rovers and Jeeps during the 1960s.

The UK-made Mayflower PTO drum winch is similar in configuration to other PTO winches and spools the cable onto its horizontal drum.

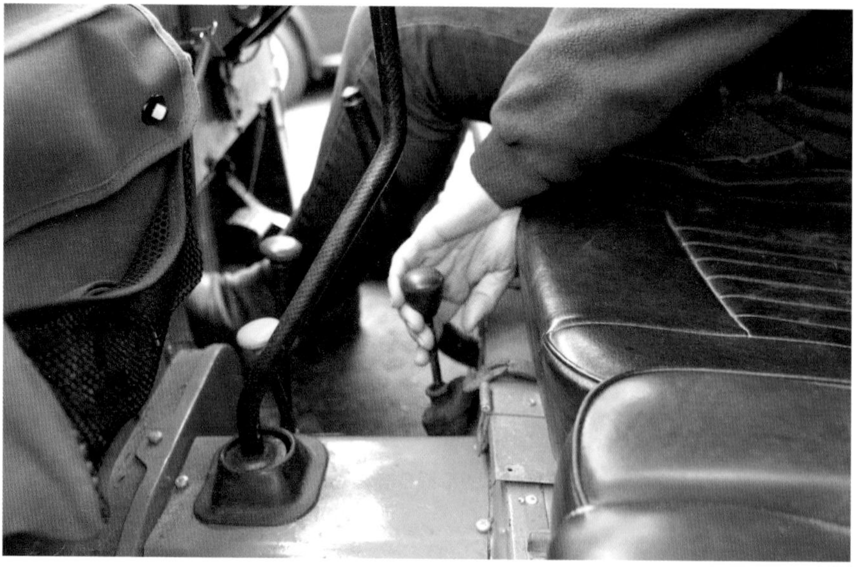

Handbrake on, engine running, transfer case in neutral, gear lever in neutral, engage PTO (as here), release handbrake and engage gear – first to winch in, reverse to winch out.

This PTO winch on this British Army Land Rover is a Turner of Wolverhapton unit and is being used for self-recovery of the stuck 4x4. It is using another Land Rover as an anchor point, although this may require further anchoring if it is not to be dragged towards the stuck vehicle.

use of Koenig winches on the now-famous Series One Station Wagons of the Oxford and Cambridge universities' First Overland expedition.

Superwinch, founded in 1970, was in Tualtin, Oregon, and Warn, founded in 1948, was in Seattle, Washington. All made 4x4 winches in the USA, while in England, Fairey, later FW Winches Ltd, made a similar configuration of a mechanical PTO drum winch. European PTO winch makers include Sepson, and Mercedes Benz for the Unimog.

The PTO winch is a handy tool on occasions, but because of the nature of the PTO controls and the location of the winch and fairlead, it does require two people for safe use and to overcome the problem that the operator cannot see the cable as it spools onto the drum.

## ELECTRIC WINCHES

Warn Industries is most synonymous with electric 4x4 winches and was founded in 1948 by Arthur Warn in Seattle, Washington. The Warn winch,

Y442 DEP
DEFENDER
SUPERWINCH

*Above*: This Jeep TJ Wrangler is fitted with a Warn 12v electrical winch.

*Opposite*: A Superwinch electric winch installed on a Land Rover Defender is being used for self-recovery.

developed in 1959, was said to be the first winch designed for recreational use. Warn added to its product range throughout the 1970s and 1980s, with numerous electric and hydraulic winches, including the famous 8274 unit, and the company's innovative features included the industry's first three-stage planetary gear train and free-spooling clutch.

## TIRFOR WINCH

Tirfor winches are portable devices that can be used to lift and pull heavy loads. They are also known as cable pullers and Tirfor hand-winches. Hand-operated, they can be used with unlimited lengths of wire rope and are available with load capacities from 800kg to 3200kg. The Tirfor is designed to pull the wire cable through a pair of mechanically operated jaws actuated by manually cranking a lever backwards and forwards, thus pulling it through the jaws at precise intervals.

A Tirfor hand-winch being used to assist with the recovery of a Land Rover. The operator is moving the lever to winch the cable in.

## EXTRA EQUIPMENT

A selection of extra equipment facilitates convenient winching and generally includes shackles in both bow and D-shapes, a selection of tree strops of varying lengths and snatch blocks that can be used to change the direction of pull or reduce the load by reducing the gearing during extreme pulls. Good-quality equipment, including, strips, shackles, lifting rings and 'snatch' pulley blocks are all marked with maximum load capacities to enable safe working practices.

A winch cable damper is a safety device used during winching to prevent the cable from scything through the air and injuring someone if it snaps under load. The damper is draped over the winch cable so that gravity will absorb the cable's energy in the case of it snapping.

The necessary extra equipment generally required for winching recoveries of stuck 4x4s. Pictured are bow- and D-shaped shackles, tree strops, a snatch block and work gloves.

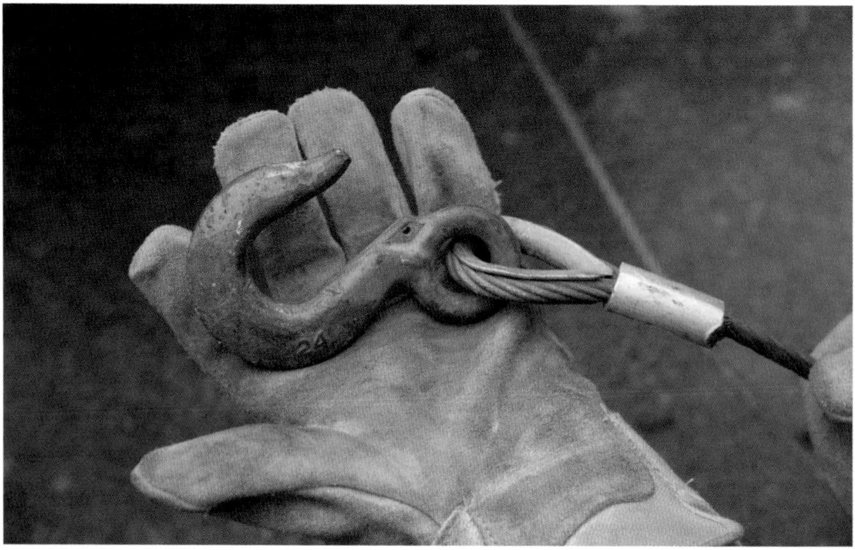

Some cables have the hook attached in an eye like this, while others require it to be shackled to the eye to enable other forms of attachment such as a lifting eye.

Lifting rings like this are rated for huge loads and very useful in winching situations where a hook cannot be safely attached, such as on a 50mm towball or NATO jaw hitch.

The winch cable needs to be spooled on neatly and in layers to preserve it, otherwise it can become jammed on itself or damaged by crushing under load. A steel winch cable should be maintained in good condition and lubricated, as it can rust and become weakened. This fairlead's upper roller has been previously bent under excessive load.

Dynaline synthetic winch rope is made with Dyneema fibre and is light-weight and high-strength. It has been designed as a replacement for the traditional steel cables that are used on recovery vehicle and 4×4 winches. Dynaline can offer quicker and safer winch deployment and recovery. It helps eliminate the dangers of recoil when a steel cable fails.

Hawse fairleads are simple, straightforward guides used to lead the cable or rope to the winch drum. They protect and reduce wear on the rope and at the same time protect the winch from unnecessary damage.

# WINCHING TECHNIQUES

## DOUBLE-LINE PULLS

The gearing of the winch increases with the number of layers of cable on the winch drum, a snatch block can be used to double-line out more cable to reduce the gearing and achieve heavier pulls. Attach the winch hook to the vehicle's tow hook, have the cable running through a snatch block and disengage the winch clutch. Then, using the snatch block, pull out enough cable to reach the chosen anchor point. Secure the snatch block to the anchor point with a tree strap and a shackle and attach the shackle to both ends of the strap, being careful not to over-tighten the shackle pin (tighten and back-off half a turn). Once the winch drive is engaged, this almost halves the gear ratio by increasing mechanical advantage and thus increasing pulling power.

## HAND SIGNALS

Where winching or winch recovery involves two people – a driver controlling the winch and an assistant ensuring that the cable is spooling properly – clear and agreed visual hand signals should be used. The driver should be able see both the assistant's hands prior to engaging the winch.

Generally accepted signals from the assistant are as follows:

- **Steering:** hold arms out with thumbs up and tilt hands in the direction required.
- **Winching in:** hold a forefinger in the air above shoulder height and describe small circles to indicate movement of the winch drum.
- **Winching out:** hold a forefinger pointing down and describe small circles at waist height to indicate allowing more cable to spool off the winch drum.
- **Stopping the winch:** a clenched fist, palm to driver, held high enough for driver to see.

Hand signals between the winch operator/driver and the assistant need to be clear and unambiguous. Here, the assistant gives the signal for winching in. Holding a forefinger in the air, he describes small circles to indicate movement of the winch.

This photograph from the 1992 Camel Trophy in Guyana shows a tricky winching operation where the Land Rover Defender 110 being recovered has a double-line pull rigged from its own winch. A single line pull is rigged from the Land Rover behind it to assist. The assistants helping to stop the Land Rover falling on its side are not standing in the safest position if a cable snaps.

## TRIPLE-LINE PULLS

Triple-line pulls use the same techniques as the double-line but lower the gearing and increase mechanical advantage further. Select a second mounting position on your vehicle for the second snatch block, as close to the winch as possible, and be ready to attach it with a shackle. Run the cable through the snatch block at the first anchor point and back to the vehicle and the second snatch block. Put the cable through the second snatch block and secure it with the shackle, then run the cable to the final anchor point where it can be secured with a tree strop and shackle. The number of snatch blocks can be increased further, and each time the mechanical advantage will be increased.

This 1996 Camel Trophy photograph from Kalimantan in Borneo shows a Land Rover 110 being recovered with a triple line pull. The cable runs from the winch to an anchor point (where a snatch block is deployed) and back to the vehicle, where another snatch block is connected to a recovery point, and finally back to another anchor point.

## CHANGING PULLING DIRECTION

Snatch blocks can also be used with carefully chosen anchor points to maintain a straight-line pull. As far as possible, all winching operations should have a straight line from the winch to the vehicle being pulled. This will minimise the wire rope collecting on one side of the drum, adversely affecting pulling efficiency and potentially damaging the cable. A snatch block, secured to a point directly in front of the vehicle, will enable the pulling direction to be varied while allowing the cable to spool properly onto the winch drum.

## 20 TIPS FOR SAFE WINCHING

1. Winch from proper vehicle anchor points and do not hook onto bumpers, spring hangers or axle casings. Check the condition of the vehicle's anchor points and be sure that any anchor point is strong enough to withstand the load applied. Keep a check on the anchor points during winching, as under heavy load a failure can have disastrous consequences.

Wire cable runs through the fairlead where the rollers turn as cable runs over them. Take care not to let the cable pile up if the winch pull isn't exactly straight, as can often be the case.

2. Wear gloves and do not let wire or synthetic winch cables slide through bare hands. This eliminates the possibility of cuts caused by slivers from broken strands or friction burns.

Industrial leather gloves should be worn when handling the cable, as snapped strands can cause injuries to the operator's hands while spooling cable back onto the drum.

3. On starting to winch, take in any slack in the cable prior to taking the strain. This will reduce the chance of damage to the winch or wire rope from shock loadings. Don't allow the cable to pile up on the drum at one side until it jams or, when spooling in, the hook to be dragged into the fairlead.
4. Stand well clear of wire rope and load during winching operations. Insist that helpers keep a safe distance from the cable (and any snatch block in use) and away from the back of a vehicle being winched up an incline.
5. Never stand astride or step over a taut cable during winching. A winch 'blanket' laid over the cable midway between the winch and the anchor point helps absorb the energy of a cable if it snaps under load.
6. Check that when ground anchors are used, or another vehicle is used as an anchor, they remain firm throughout the duration of the pull. Use vehicle ground anchors when recovering another vehicle, otherwise the recovering vehicle maybe pulled towards the stuck one.
7. Do not handle the winch cable or rigging during winching operations or touch a cable or its hook while they are under load. When a winch is not in operation, there may still be a considerable load on the cable.
8. Stop winching when the hook is at least a safe distance away from the winch fairlead and take in the final length in small increments to avoid accidents. Keep hands and fingers clear of the cable when winching, and do not put your finger through the hook when reeling in the cable.

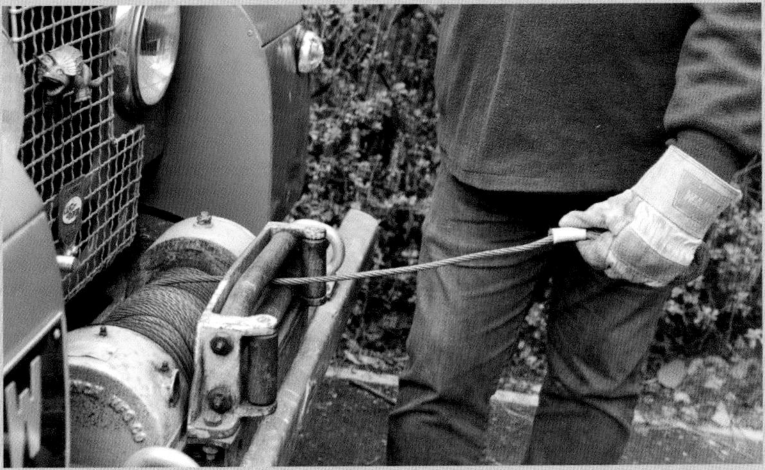

By the time the cable is this far in, the operator cannot see the end of the cable and so must watch for the assistant's hand signal of when to stop to avoid the hook going into the fairlead.

9. Do not operate a winch with fewer than five turns of the cable on the drum to ensure it does not detach from the winch drum under load, as the rope fastener will not support a heavy load.
10. Ensure that the rope is correctly respooled onto the winch drum after use. Inspect and carefully re-wind the wire cable after use. Crushed, pinched and frayed sections reduce the cable's tensile strength. Cables should be replaced when any form of damage is evident.

This, for example, can cause the wire to become crushed under load. If the cable is crushed, strands can break, meaning it can injure the assistant or break under load.

11. To avoid cable damage, do not put a cable round an anchor point and hook it onto itself, as this will damage the cable.
12. Do not use the winch to tow another vehicle, as winch mechanisms are not designed for this and sudden jerking may cause the cable to fail.
13. Do not exceed the capacity of the winch. Using a pulley or snatch block to double the line pull will almost halve the load on the winch and the wire rope. Doing this is the most important aid to successful winching, after the winch itself, and can be used to increase the pulling power of the winch or for indirect pulls. Pulley blocks can be deployed in two ways – attached to the vehicle to be recovered, or secured to an anchor point. The anchor point, when used, must be secure and able to withstand the load necessary to recover the vehicle.

14. It is good practice to use a tree strop to protect the trunk when a tree is used as an anchor point. A shackle should always be used when attaching winch hooks to nylon straps.

Good-quality equipment including, strips, shackles, lifting rings and 'snatch' pulley blocks are all marked with maximum load capacities to enable safe working practices.

15. Hand signals from the winch operator to the vehicle driver need to be clear and unambiguous during winching operations when the duo may not be able to hear each other speak as a result of distance or engine noise.

The driver pays attention to the commands communicated to him through hand signals and the assistant makes sure that his signals are clearly visible.

16. Synthetic rope is a suitable product for vehicle recovery situations. It is light in weight, easy to handle, does not develop broken strands like steel cable and doesn't store as much potential energy when under load. Synthetic rope can be used on a winch designed for steel cable. It can have a breaking strain of up to 30 per cent more than steel cable of equal diameter, because it is constructed out of a unique ultra-high-molecular-weight polyethylene (UHMWPE) material.

17. Before using an electric winch, inspect the control lead for cracks, pinched wiring, fraying or loose connections. A short-circuit could cause the winch to operate as soon as it is plugged in. When the control lead is plugged in, keep it clear of the drum, fairlead area, cable and any rigging. Only plug the control lead in when you need to use the winch and store the control lead in a clean, dry part of the vehicle where it cannot be damaged. When using the remote control from inside the vehicle, pass the lead through the window to avoid trapping it in the door.

Here, the winch operator uses the electric winch control through the window of a Land Rover Discovery to avoid trapping it in the door.

18. If the winch is powered from the vehicle's battery, take care that this is not discharged so the engine cannot be restarted to avoid becoming stranded. It is recommended that the engine be kept running during winching operations to provide charging current to the battery. Avoid overheating the winch motor during extended winching by pausing at reasonable intervals to allow the winch motor to cool.

It is advised to keep the vehicle's engine running when an electric winch is being used to avoid the battery losing its charge and not being able to restart the vehicle.

19. Avoid continuous winching pulls from extreme angles, as this will cause the cable to pile up at one end of the winch drum. Where possible, aim to get the cable as straight as possible compared to the direction of the vehicle. Snatch blocks can be used to help achieve this.
20. Isolate the winch, either mechanically (disengage the PTO lever) or electrically (switch the power off), before putting hands near the fairlead or winch cable drum, to avoid accidents. Do not operate the winch clutch if there is a load on the cable. Unspool it a bit before releasing the clutch to free the spool to release tension.

A Swiss Team Land Rover 110 is winched out of trouble during a Camel Trophy event. Tree strops have been looped around the roll cage to enable winch cables and snatch blocks to be affixed to stop the vehicle toppling off the track.

# NAVIGATION

The road, in J.R.R. Tolkien's words, 'goes ever on and on,' so you'll need a map to know where you're going. In these days of pocket-sized Satnavs and Global Positioning Systems (GPS), many people seem to be turning their backs on the paper map. This is a shame in many ways, because, although the electronic devices will get you where you're going, there is a mass of other information on a map. If a journey involves travelling in remote areas, it is always worth taking a map and compass as a backup to a portable GPS, as well as a mobile phone, portable phone charger and GPS unit. The wilderness rule of thumb is simple: always carry a compass with you.

GPS is a satellite-based radio-navigation system owned and operated by the United States government and made freely accessible to anyone with a GPS receiver. It is one of the global navigation satellite systems (GNSS) that provide geolocation and time information to a GPS receiver anywhere on or near the earth where there is an unobstructed line of sight to four or more GPS satellites. Obstacles such as mountains and buildings can block the relatively weak GPS signals – a very good reason to carry a map. GPS does not require the user to transmit any data, and operates independently of any telephonic or internet reception, though these can enhance the practicality of the GPS positioning information. GPS provides critical positioning capabilities to military, civilian and commercial users around the world.

Accurate and up-to-date maps of some areas may not exist, and if there are few significant landmarks or few road networks, navigation can be difficult.

This problem can be exacerbated in snow or desert conditions, where tracks can be covered by drifting snow or sand. Large lakes and rivers can be used to help pinpoint a position, but, on the ground, there may be small lakes and rivers that are not on a map (depending on scale) so cannot be relied on to assist with navigation.

Geography also offers clues for navigation; in eastern Canada, snowdrifts point to the northwest, and in Scandinavia, striations on rock and cliff caused by glaciers run northwest to southeast because of prevailing weather conditions. Many trees are bushier on their south side, and trees bend away from a prevailing wind that frequently blows from the west.

*Above*: Eighteen nations participated in the competitive 2006 Land Rover G4 Challenge. Turkish and Italian competitors prepare for a competitive orienteering challenge.

*Opposite*: The Global Positioning System (GPS) is a satellite-based radio-navigation system operated by the United States Space Force for the United States government. It provides geolocation and time information to GPS receivers anywhere on Earth when there is an unobstructed line of sight to four or more GPS satellites.

GARMIN
GOTO
IN
QUIT
OUT
GPS III
PAGE
MENU
ENTER
MARK
N 330 345 N 015 030 N
TRIP TIMER
45:32
SUNRISE
07:07
SUNSET
18:10
SPEED
0.0
TRIP ODOM
2284
16:55:30
21-FEB-01
AVG SPEED
50.2
N 37.60309°
W006.28319°
GARMIN

# COMPASS

The use of a compass is a common way to determine direction, but remember, the magnetic field becomes weaker the nearer the magnetic poles, and it can be affected by other objects. A UK example is the magnetic deviation in the Cuillin Hills range of rocky mountains located on the Isle of Skye in Scotland. The deviation is very variable, so it is not a good idea to rely on a compass there. In some parts, the compass wanders, in others it spins if lifted from or lowered towards the rock. It is, therefore, important to make sure that the compass is not affected by iron fragments in the ground, or the presence of vehicles.

An angle is the opening between two lines meeting at a point. Angles are usually spoken of as being of a number of degrees. The degrees are measured

Even the most basic magnetic compass will indicate directions used for navigation and geographic orientation. It comprises a magnetised needle that pivots to point towards magnetic north.

on the circumference, the centre of which is on the point of the angle. There are 360 degrees in the circumference of a circle. The surface of the earth is so divided north and south by the parallels of latitude, which are numbered from the equator each way, and east and west by the meridians of longitude, which number from Greenwich, England. These can be seen on almost any map. A small pocket compass will be accurate enough for 4x4 navigation purposes but is of little value if a person does not know how to use it. It will not tell you in what direction to go but, when the needle is allowed to swing freely on its pivot, the coloured end always points to magnetic north, and it is this that aids navigation.

Magnetic north is the location where the Earth's magnetic field points vertically downward. The direction of magnetic north changes with time and location on the earth's surface. True north is also known as geographic north and is the direction along the surface of the earth that ends in the location of the North Pole. True north lies a degree or more to either side of magnetic north. In the west of the US, for example, the needle will be attracted slightly to the east, while on the Atlantic coast it will swing slightly to the west of true north. This magnetic variation need not always be taken into account when absolute accuracy is not required or when navigation is being achieved from magnetic north bearings. Grid north is the direction of a grid system, usually the grid associated with the map projection. Maps published by the United States Geographical Survey (USGS) and the British Ordnance Survey (OS) contain a diagrammatic north arrow that shows all three norths.

Confusion can come from the names of the angles between true north, magnetic north and grid north and the definition of magnetic variation (also known as declination). Some sources have magnetic variation as the horizontal angle between magnetic north and grid north. However, the OS and the British Geological Association have magnetic as the angle between magnetic north and true north. The angle between magnetic north and grid north is the grid magnetic angle (GMA), and it is this angle that needs to be applied when converting between magnetic and grid bearings.

NAVIGATION

With the aid of a compass, maps can be orientated so that north on the map corresponds to north in the terrain. This means the map's topography correlates to the visible landscape topography.

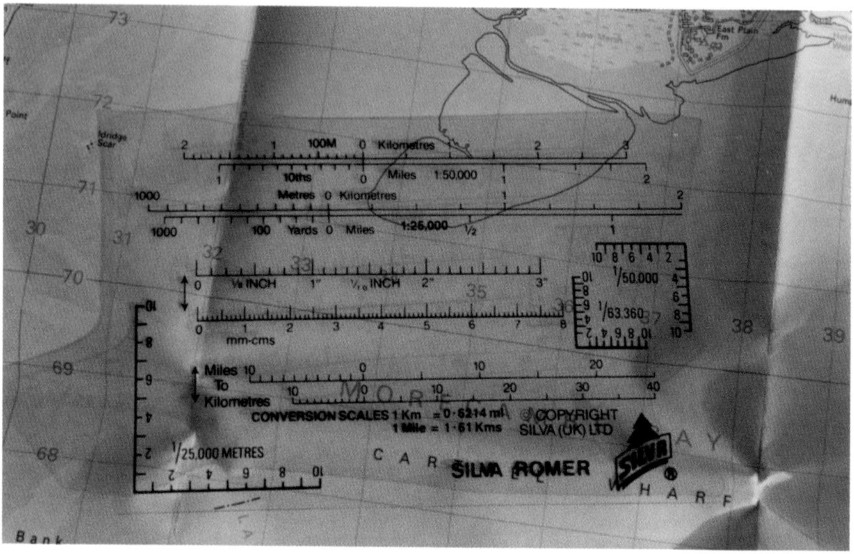


The 'romer' is a device that aids in plotting accurate positions and map references on a map. The one pictured has grids for both 1:25,000- and 1:50,000-scale maps. This Silva-made item is square, while the Don Barrow one for rally navigators is teardrop shaped.

There are numerous types of magnetic compass. Pictured is a brass prismatic compass that incorporates a triangular glass prism so that the compass can be read while taking a bearing on a landmark. Also shown are two examples of the baseplate-type compass used for navigation with a map.

A compass can be used to follow a route in a specific direction; hold the compass level so that the needle swings free. Take a bearing on a landmark, such as a prominent tree, high cliff or other conspicuous object in the direction of travel, and go directly to this object. Consult the compass frequently when making a detour or when the landmark passes out of sight. When this marker is reached, select another farther on and continue to travel, always picking out new marks along the bearing indicated by the compass.

## COMPASS TYPES

Navigation aids have taken many forms over the years. From the compass to the GPS to now even mobile devices, there is no shortage of navigational tools. Though GPS and smartphones are reliable, it is still advisable to carry a compass and know how to use it, as a backup potentially lifesaving form of navigation.

### PRISMATIC COMPASS

A prismatic compass is a navigation and surveying instrument that is extensively used to find out the bearing of the direction of travel. The name prismatic compass is used because the compass includes a prism that is used for taking bearings accurately.

### BASEPLATE COMPASS

Baseplate compasses are great all-around hiking and travel compasses. They often have a clear baseplate, which makes them great for map use, as they can be laid across the map, looked through and lined up as required. The more expensive baseplate compasses generally have slightly larger capsules with longer needles, improving the readable accuracy of the compass. More expensive baseplate compasses also add special features like adjustable declination, map scales, a magnifying lens, luminous points, cut-outs for map marking and even a global needle. A famous worldwide brand is Silva, which has manufactured baseplate compasses for orienteering, outdoor life, adventures and boating since 1933. The Kjellström brothers, Silva's founders, invented the first liquid-filled compass and revolutionised navigation and set a global standard. The liquid created resistance, which prevented the needle from spinning, enabling the compass to be read more quickly.

## LENSATIC COMPASS

The term 'lensatic' comes from the fact that there is a lens on the rear side of the compass that aids in the orienteering process. A lensatic compass is often referred to as a 'military compass' and is typically used by the US Armed Forces. The lensatic compass comprises different parts compared to a baseplate compass, namely a cover, base, and reading lens. The cover protects the compass but also incorporates the sighting wire that helps determine direction. The base is the compass dial, bezel and the thumb loop used for stability to achieve an accurate reading. It is used in a similar way to a baseplate compass, but there are also slight differences – including how you hold a lensatic compass.

A liquid-filled baseplate, also known as a protractor or orienteering compass. The string lanyard means the compass can be carried around the user's neck.

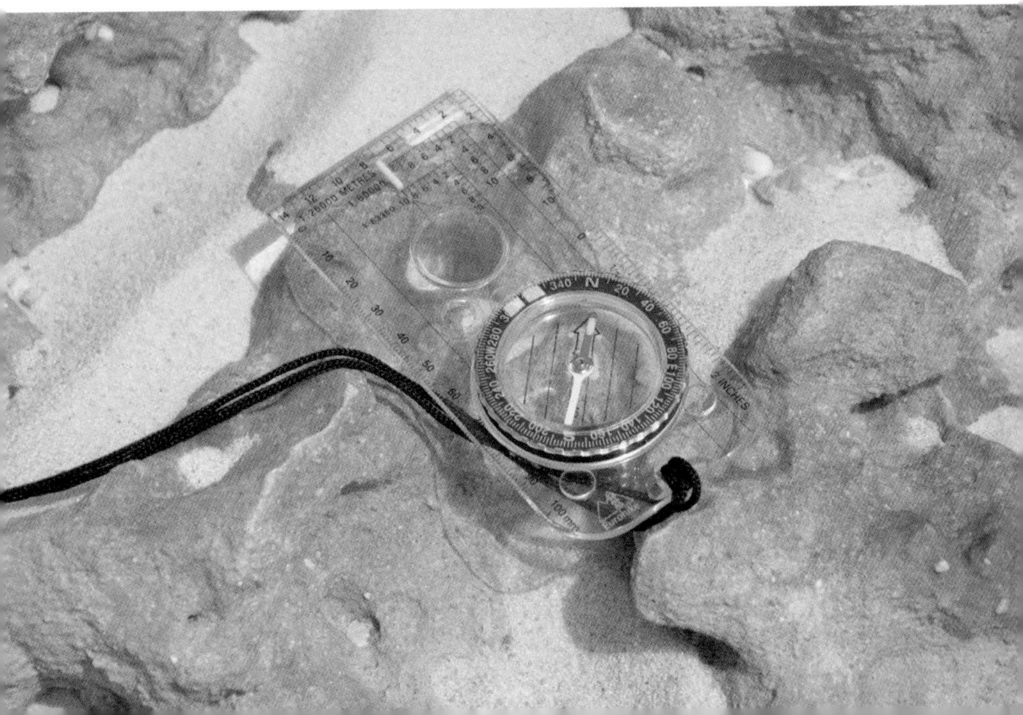

US Army personnel on a training exercise using the Cammenga 3H (US M-1950) military lensatic compass. It does not use a liquid-filled capsule as a damping mechanism, but relies on electromagnetic induction to control oscillation of its magnetised disc.

## DIRECTION FROM THE SUN

There are two ways to determine direction by the sun; firstly, at noon in the Northern Hemisphere, the shadows fall to the north of objects, and in the Southern Hemisphere to the south. Secondly, direction can be estimated by using a watch with hands. It can be used as compass on a clear day by pointing the hour hand to the sun. In northern latitudes, point the hour hand towards the sun and an imaginary line between the hour hand and the '12' on the watch face will point due south. In southern latitudes, point the '12' towards the sun and the imaginary line between the hour hand and the '12' will point north. Bear in mind that the sun may be obscured by clouds, making it more difficult to read the direction.

# MAKE A 'SUN COMPASS'

Because the sun always rises in the east and sets in the west, shadows invariably move in the opposite direction. This is something that that you can use to your advantage to plot true north at any time when the sun is shining. Collect a few straight sticks (canes are used here for demonstration purposes). Push the first into the centre of a fairly level area of ground then mark the tip of its shadow with a second stick. The sun moves east to west at about 15 degrees per hour, so wait for 10–15 minutes until the shadow has moved a few inches and mark the location of the tip of the shadow again. Finally, use a third stick or draw a straight line in the sand or dirt from the first marker to the second. This line points from east to west, so by remembering the clockwise 'Never Eat Shredded Wheat' for north, east, south, west, it is possible to determine where north and south are because north (Never) is at 90 degrees above the line and south (Shredded) is 90 degrees below it.

To find direction, push the first stick (yellow tape) into the sand, mark its shadow with a second (green tape), wait for the shadow to move and mark the shadow again with the third stick (blue tape) and the line between the second and third sticks, shown here with a fourth stick (red tape), points from east to west.

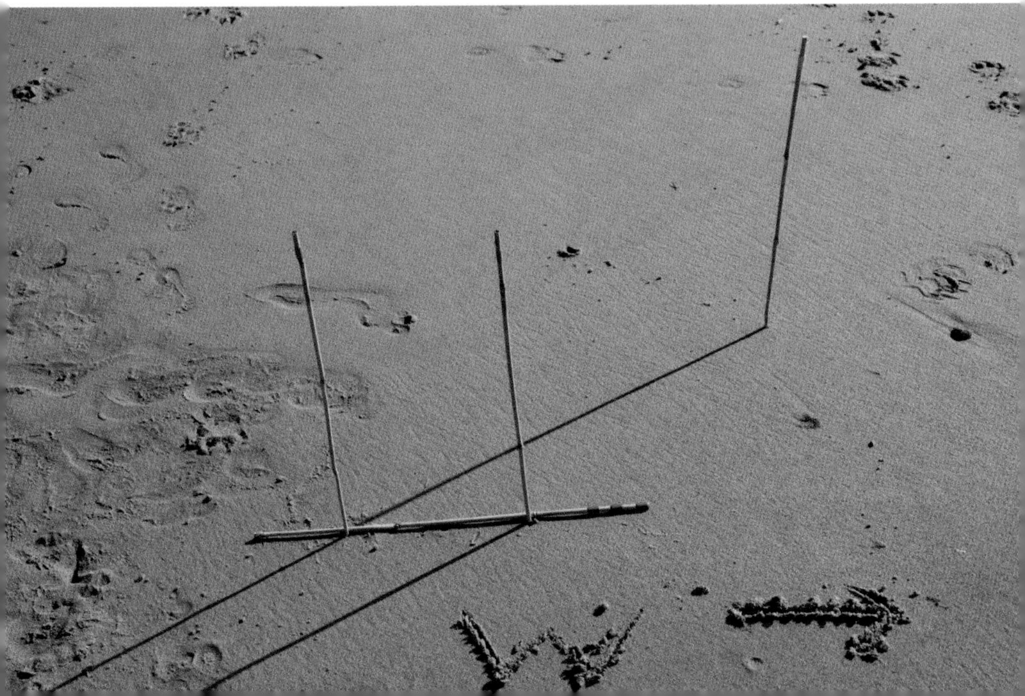

## DIRECTION FROM THE STARS

In the northern hemisphere, the North Star can be used to determine true north. It can easily be found by its position relative to the Big Dipper (US, Canada) or the Plough (UK, Ireland) asterism (a pattern or group of stars) that can be seen in the night sky. In latitudes of less than 70 degrees when travelling north, the North Star is a good steering mark, as its bearing usually ranges between one and 2.5 degrees from true north. In latitudes above 70 degrees, the North Star is too high in the sky to be reliably used for direction finding.

In the Southern Hemisphere, the Crux, a constellation of the southern sky that is centred on four bright stars in a cross-shaped asterism, commonly known as the Southern Cross, helps find the general direction of south. The two stars forming the long axis of the cross are the pointers. From the lower of these, extend the line five times its own length to an imaginary point. This point is the general direction of south, look vertically down to the horizon and select something to aim for. As with navigating from the sun, this technique requires the stars to be visible in the sky and not obscured by cloud.

## MAPPING MINUTIAE

British OS maps in particular have a charm all their own. The 'one-inch' maps and their metric 1:50,000 derivatives have long been the map of choice for recreationalists in Britain, and the covers of each series of their updated and revised editions entice with the promise of adventures to come. Later came metrication and the appearance of the purple-covered 1:50,000 (1.25in to one mile)-scale maps. The purple-covered maps endure to this day as the ubiquitous OS Landranger series of maps, the covers of which also now incorporate a colour photograph of somewhere relevant to the map. The history and the name go back much further, 'Necessity is the mother of invention', is a well-worn saying, but a true one. What's more, history proves that, on numerous occasions, the specific necessity was defence.

Planning a route at the table of a cafe in Morocco comes with promises of desert adventures ahead.

The flat expanse of the bonnet/hood of a 4x4 is a convenient height to spread out maps.

It was the 1745 Jacobite Highland uprising that threatened English King George II that began the accurate mapping of Britain. The King commissioned a military survey of the Scottish Highlands in 1746, as well as a considerable amount of road building. The need to map more of Britain for strategic purposes came later that century, when there were concerns that wars with the French might cross the English Channel. Therefore, the government ordered its defence ministry, the Board of Ordnance, to begin a survey of England's south coast. Work began in June 1791, as surveyors began mapping southern Britain, working from a baseline that William Roy, the surveyor of the Highlands, had measured several years earlier. The first 1in-to-the-mile OS map of Kent was published in 1801. By 1820, roughly a third of England and Wales had been mapped. Although this might seem like slow progress in these days of electronic hardware, in order to do so, Major Thomas Colby had walked 586 miles on a 22-day reconnaissance expedition in 1819.

One aspect that fascinates is the degree of detail that can be found on OS maps: different symbols for churches with spires and those with towers; whether railways were single- or double-track; and whether wooded areas contained coniferous or deciduous trees and so on. Geographical features could be imagined from the closeness of the contour lines, and whether there were the symbols for rocky outcrops or not. Most of these features are shown on the current editions, although the distinction between single and double railway tracks is no longer made, and, reflecting changing times and the ongoing quest for accuracy, churches with spires are now described as a 'current or former place of worship with spire, minaret or dome'. As you might imagine, the rights of way information has also changed, as new categories of rights of way have been created and others have disappeared – specifically Byways Open to All Traffic (BOAT) and Roads Used as Public Paths (RUPP), respectively.

A prolific producer of maps of Britain and Ireland was Scottish publisher John Bartholomew and Son Ltd of Duncan Street, Edinburgh. This eponymous company was founded by John Bartholomew (1805–61) and, subsequently, his son and grandson made Bartholomew the important map publisher that it became. John Bartholomew Jr was credited with having pioneered the use of hypsometric tints, also known as layer colouring, on maps, in which low ground is shown in shades of green and higher ground in shades of brown, then eventually purple and finally white. His son, John George, is attributed with being the first to bring the name 'Antarctica' into popular use as the name for the southern continent, and for the adoption of red or pink as the colour for the British Empire.

Bartholomew's maps are often regarded as the poor relations of OS maps but were popular with motorists and cyclists, who preferred Bartholomew's half-inch to the mile scale over the one-inch OS map. The suggestions for revisions by the Cyclists Touring Club were acknowledged on the maps in the heyday of that organisation. It is said that the army also preferred the half-inch scale, but the OS was only persuaded to take this scale seriously when it was losing sales to Bartholomew. The company was notable for its varied output of maps and atlases for academic, commercial and travel purposes, including the popular 62-sheet Half-Inch to One Mile map series of Great Britain, which evolved into the 1:100,000 National map series in the 1970s. This series was eventually discontinued, owing largely to competition from the state-financed OS. In 1989, the firm merged with the Glasgow publisher Collins, as part of the multinational HarperCollins Publishers under Rupert Murdoch's News International Corporation.

Lots of old maps were published by Geographia Ltd, of 167 Fleet Street, London. Geographia Ltd was founded in 1911 by Alexander Gross (1879–1958), a Hungarian immigrant who had come to Britain in the early 20th century. It was a prolific publisher of globes, maps and atlases from the early 1900s to the late 1980s. Geographia published numerous popular roadmaps of the period and specialised in producing atlases, special-edition maps (including licenced editions of foreign maps) and tourist maps of London and other cities and towns. Finally, it was absorbed into Collins Bartholomew, the cartographic division of HarperCollins, but, of the map companies in Britain during the last century, Geographia Ltd can be considered the third largest after OS and Bartholomew. The British Isles mapping arm of HarperCollins (formerly Geographia Ltd) was based in Cheltenham until 2009.

*Above*: During the 20th century, the Ordnance Survey (OS) produced a huge variety of types of maps in a variety of scales, including the famous 'one-inch' series at one-inch to the mile and the later 1:25,000 and 1:50,000 metric versions.

*Left*: Pictured here are 1950s and 1970s editions of the one-inch series.

The metric versions of the one-inch OS maps were the 1:50,000 Landranger maps with distinctive purple covers. These and the 1:25,000 Explorer maps are popular for 4x4 use.

Bartholomew was a 20th century publisher of maps and its half-inch to the mile series of maps was particularly popular for decades.

OS Ireland has evolved from the Ordnance Survey Office, which was established in 1824, later becoming a state body under the Ordnance Survey Ireland Act 2001. Its current maps are the Discovery series.

## FRANCE

There was, and still is, a bewildering selection of maps of France available, with different scales, size of area, and regional and national locations covered. Michelin maps are produced on behalf of the famous tyre company; they were first issued more than a century ago, and a version with the famous yellow covers first appeared in the early 1950s. For 30 years prior to this, the maps had orange and blue covers, and since then there have been eight or nine series, differentiated by the evolving cover designs that parallel mapping updates. The tyre connection is clear, and the famous trademark 'Michelin Man' appears on maps from 1921 onwards. Michelin maps have a visually effective, airbrushed style of marking the topography of mountains and forests in areas such as the Alps. Different from British OS maps, it does not take long to get used to them, and one can both navigate accurately and see the wealth of detail contained on each map. Numerous versions were printed by all sides in World War Two, and the US Army even reprinted the Michelin Guide to France to help its troops navigate during the liberation – a scene involving a Michelin guide appears in the film *Kelly's Heroes*. Michelin hasn't ignored its heritage and sells numerous historical maps, and, because France is blessed with rivers and mountains, the company produces maps for cyclists and canoeists as well. Michelin looked beyond France from its earliest days, so maps of Great Britain and other European countries are plentiful, as are maps of North Africa, the latter is because of France's former colonial associations with various North African countries and its proximity south across the Mediterranean.

Institut Géographique National (IGN) maps are France's equivalent of the UK's OS. The IGN's aim is to produce, maintain and disseminate geographic information in France, and the organisation has been involved in all cartography-related operations in France and its territories since 1940. As a result, it offers a vast selection of maps including more than 2,000 maps of France in a variety of scales. All IGN maps feature an easy-to-use key in English, French and German. There are similar organisations in Belgium (Institut Géographique National/Nationaal Geografisch Instituut) and Spain (Instituto Geográfico Nacional).

Primarily a tyre manufacturer, Michelin is also renowned internationally for its maps. It began producing maps to encourage motorists to travel further afield in their cars.

As motoring became more popular, Michelin expanded its range of maps by widening the range of places covered. Currently, Michelin is widely respected for its cartographic output.

Institut Géographique National (IGN) maps are detailed French maps designed to produce, maintain and disseminate reference geographic information in France. IGN offers more than 2,000 maps of France in a variety of scales.

The Instituto Geográfico Nacional produces topographic maps of Spain at a 1:25,000 scale. Corresponding Michelin maps are at a smaller scale, but both prove useful for navigation.

## THE UNITED STATES

Topographic maps became a signature product of the United States Geological Survey (USGS) because they proved to be a useful tool for viewing the nation's vast landscape. The USGS was entrusted with the responsibility for mapping the country in 1879 and remains the primary civilian mapping agency of the US. Its best-known maps are the 1:24,000-scale (a non-metric scale virtually unique to the US) topographic maps, also known as '7.5-minute quadrangles'. From approximately 1947 to 1992, more than 55,000 7.5-minute maps were made to cover the conterminous 48 states. Each of these maps covers an area bounded by two lines of latitude and two lines of longitude, spaced 7.5 minutes apart. Because the area covered by each map varies with the latitude of its represented location owing to convergence of the meridians, at lower latitudes, near 30 degrees north, a 7.5-minute quadrangle contains an area of about 64 square miles (166km$^2$). At 49 degrees north latitude, 49 square miles (127km$^2$) are contained within a quadrangle of that size. Similar maps at varying scales were also produced for Hawaii, the US territories and areas of Alaska near Anchorage, Fairbanks and Prudhoe Bay. The 7.5-minute series was declared complete in 1992, and at that time was the only uniform map series that covered the US in considerable detail. As a unique, non-metric map scale, the 1:24,000 scale requires a separate and specialised Romer scale for plotting map positions accurately.

Map revision continued through the 1990s, until the last printed USGS topographic maps were published in 2006. In 2009, a new USGS quadrangle topographic map series, US Topo, was published. These are modelled on the 7.5-minute series, but derived from geographic information system (GIS) data. Both US Topo and Historical Topographic Map Collection (HTMC) maps can be downloaded free of charge through several USGS websites.

The United States remains almost the only developed country in the world without a standardised civilian topographic map series in the standard 1:25,000 or 1:50,000 metric scales, making coordination difficult in border regions. The US military does, however, issue 1:50,000 scale topographic maps of the continental United States, though only for use by members of its armed forces. The USGS has produced various specialist maps in a variety of scales. These include county maps, maps of special interest areas, such as national parks, and areas of scientific interest.

There is another type of US map that is commonly available – the 'gas station' maps from the likes of Texaco and Rand McNally. Rand McNally's maps predate the advent of the car; in 1856, William Rand opened a printing shop in Chicago, and, in 1858, an Irish immigrant, Andrew McNally, got a job in Rand's shop. By 1868, the duo had formed a partnership, Rand McNally & Co., to print tickets and timetables for Chicago's railways. In 1899, Rand left the company to pursue other interests, and McNally became president. His family would run the business for the next century. In 1904, Rand McNally's first automobile roadmap, the snappily titled *New Automobile Roadmap of New York City and Vicinity* was published.

Noted aviator Charles Lindbergh used Rand McNally railroad maps to navigate overland at the start of his historic flight across the Atlantic in 1927. Then, in 1939, within 24 hours of Germany's invasion of Poland, stores across the US sold out of Rand McNally's map of Europe. In 1960, the first full-colour Rand McNally road atlas was published, and the company began creating maps digitally in 1982. Then, in 2013, as the printed road atlas celebrated its 90th edition, Rand McNally launched iPad and eBook versions.

Rand McNally and other major mapmakers, such as General Drafting and H. M. Gousha, dominated the mapmaking industry. By the 1920s, branded roadmaps produced by these companies were being given away free as a way of advertising, and often included attraction and historic facts to make them more appealing to travellers. The Great Depression of the 1930s encouraged roadmap giveaways as companies attempted to attract business; oil companies including Texaco, Socony-Vacuum (later Mobil),

American maps such as these Moab trail maps (left) and National Geographic branded maps are compiled from USGS mapping information. The USGS has been mapping the US since 1879.

A selection of Rand McNally roadmaps at different scales, dating from the 1970s to present.

Rand McNally is one US publisher of roadmaps, and it, alongside other US map publishers, often published maps for other brands such as the American Automobile Association and Texaco.

Esso, Standard, Chevron, Gulf and Shell all produced them. The production of free maps declined significantly during World War Two, as resources were conserved for the war effort. In the post-war boom years, promotional roadmap production soared again.

The idea of petrol/gasoline stations producing maps found favour across the Atlantic, and it seems that all the petrol companies offered them, including National Benzole, Shell, Mobil, Esso and BP. To be of use to motorists, each map covered a specific region. This meant the size of the map would cover lengthy journeys in sufficient detail to enable accurate navigation in those pre-satnav years. Different editions were printed and so reflect the advent of motorways, bypasses and ever-extending dual carriageways. Esso maps from the 1960s, for example, offer a glimpse into ancient corners of the old shires and border towns of the British Isles with welcoming cover images.

In Zagora, in the Draa River valley of southern Morocco, is this old painted sign that indicates that Tombouctou (Timbuktu) in Mali is 52 jours (days) to the south by camel.

# CAMPING

There are numerous types of camping, and each offers its own challenges and rewards. It is a convenient way to explore the great outdoors, get some fresh air and spend time with friends and family. Camping with a 4x4 is a form of car camping that differs from, for example, backpacking, in terms of how much gear you can take with you and where you camp. Camping in the great outdoors can be a great adventure or a nightmare to be survived. The difference depends mostly on one thing; what you *do* pack and what you *don't* pack. Bear in mind, most trips are remembered for the comfort of sleeping and/or the toilet facilities. Your sleeping kit, for example, might be the most expensive part of a camping set-up, but it will determine whether you love or hate a camping experience.

Car camping generally involves driving onto your campsite, and the unloading often involves structured campsites or 'glampsites' with facilities. However, camping with a 4x4 can offer an experience closer to the backpacker's back-to-basics approach because a 4x4 can take you to remote backcountry campsites that are devoid of facilities and neighbours. With a 4x4, as with car

## CAMPING ESSENTIALS

- Cooking utensils/cutlery
- Insect repellent and sunscreen
- Lighting, such as torches, and spare batteries
- Portable stove, fuel and matches
- Rubbish bags
- Sleeping bag
- Sleeping mats and folding chairs
- Tent
- Toilet paper

camping, you load up your gear, drive to your chosen camping spot, park and unload your gear from your vehicle. This is why many 4x4 campers use their vehicle as a cooking or sleeping area as well as transport for their gear. Although space is rarely a problem with 4x4s, there are minimum equipment requirements as well as luxuries, and all these can be divided into straightforward camping gear and personal gear for each person.

## REMOTE SAFETY ESSENTIALS

- Fire extinguisher, easily accessible
- First aid kit
- Flashlight and batteries, plus spares
- Maps, compass, GPS and flares
- Sat phone
- Tarp or Basha sheet

So long as you are prepared for the cold, camping can be a year-round activity.

A vintage-style camp scene with a ridge tent and a paraffin hurricane lantern. Camping technology has progressed massively in recent years.

The six members of the First Overland London to Singapore Expedition with their Land Rovers and all their equipment, including camping and cooking equipment. Note the awning stretched between the two vehicles for cooking under.

# TENT CAMPING

Make it enjoyable and stress-free! It's fair to say that camping without the right gear isn't quite as much fun as being in a dry tent after a cooked meal. Remember that you can still sleep under the stars if you want, but, if you have pitched a tent and it gets cold or wet, you can retreat into the tent. A midnight storm, unexpected snowstorm or heavy dew will otherwise leave you drenched, miserable and at risk of hypothermia. Tents come in all shapes and sizes, and it's important to choose one that's suitable for your needs. When picking one, it's a good idea to choose one that's designed for more than the number of people using it. This is easy, as tents are usually sized by person and will allow enough room to store your gear in the tent and have comfortable space to sleep.

The Vango Force 10 ridge tent was, for many years, the standard mountain tent and reputed to stand up to Force 10 winds.

When overnighting, basha sheets can work if rigged well, but full tents are better for privacy on crowded campgrounds and for protecting against bugs and rain. Some like to camp in hammocks, and versions with rainproof covers and midge nets are available, but remember you need to be going to a wooded area to use them easily, although some people sling them between two 4x4s. Bivvy bags are another option and offer a low-hassle but basic alternative to a tent. They are waterproof and windproof, and the user simply places a sleeping bag inside the bivvy bag, without the need for pegs or poles. Some bivvy bags have a small pole to keep the fabric away from the user's head, but many others do not. A bivvy bag might take a bit of getting used to, but it offers overnight shelter sleeping beneath the stars. The bivvy bag at its most basic is a plastic survival bag with the open end supported with a stick.

Camping has changed immeasurably in recent years, as more people look to the great outdoors for fun and adventure. Camping is no longer

The awning-type tent for the rear of 4x4 vehicles has long been popular. This is a 1960s type made by Carawagon to suit its line of Land Rover camper conversions.

the back-to-basics activity that it once was, and tents have evolved greatly. Dome-type ground tents are now widely available and incorporate flexible poles. Such dome tents have their origins in backpacking and make good use of modern materials and designs that ensure they are light, easy to transport and easy to pitch. Recently, they have become available in larger sizes thanks to clever design that makes them particularly good in poor weather conditions. It is much easier to find a decent tent for camping at a reasonable price if you do not have to worry about weight – a benefit of 4x4 camping.

To be comfortable in a ground tent, carefully select where you pitch it. It is important to consider the weather on an outdoors trip that will last a few days or more. In the UK, conditions can change hour to hour and will rarely be the same for a few days in a row. Choose ample flat ground to pitch a tent on in an area not likely to flood if it rains. Access to water and adequate privacy are other factors to consider. On exposed campsites, put the back of

Despite the popularity of roof tents for 4x4s, there is still a place for traditional ground camping.

The increasing popularity of motorhomes has seen the number of awning tents increase. These are useful, as the back of the vehicle can be used for cooking undercover.

Some campsites have more facilities than others!

Small-size dome tents can be pitched quickly and don't take up much room in a vehicle, thus suiting trips that involve moving on each day.

Large awning tents are suited to families and as base camp tents. Mesh fly screens are often useful.

the tent into the wind to give it more stability and try and put pegs into the ground at a 45-degree angle, although this is easier said than done on rocky sites. Also think about setting up camp; the more complicated your tent, the longer it takes to get from arrival at the campsite to relaxing by the fire.

## ROOF TENTS

Many consider rooftop tents as an alternative to tents and RVs when it comes to 4x4 camping. As a result, they have become a popular accessory for 4x4s in recent years because users are not restricted to traditional camping location options. Essentially, they can be used to camp anywhere a 4x4 can go and are not as bulky as camper vehicles. Roof tents are mounted to the

Roof tents are mounted on a 4x4 by means of its roof rack. They are folded shut for travelling, opened for sleeping and are accessed by a ladder.

Maggiolina Auto roof tents have been manufactured since the 1950s. The current Maggiolina models are spacious, comfortable and safe. There are two types of opening mechanism: crank handles and gas springs.

crossbars of a roof rack that is fastened to the roof of a 4x4 and are accessed by a fold-out ladder when being rigged for camping. Generally, they are housed in a waterproof plastic cover or a fibreglass box with a hinge to open that pulls the tent up as it does so. Many are designed so that bedding can be left in the roof tent, meaning that it does not have to be carried within the 4x4. Early examples of roof tents appeared in Europe during the 1930s, but now they are a common sight on expedition-prepared 4x4s such as Land Rovers. They are undoubtedly popular and remain expensive, so, depending on the type of 4x4 trip or camping required, it can be as practical to buy a decent ground tent.

The *Long Way Down* is a television series and book following a motorcycle journey undertaken in 2007 by Ewan McGregor and Charley Boorman, from John o' Groats in Scotland through 18 countries to Cape Town in South Africa. The support and film crew used Nissan Patrols fitted with roof tents.

A Land Rover 110 fitted with a Howling Moon roof tent and awnings. These are made in South Africa by a company with more than 40 years' experience.

## SLEEPING BAGS AND OTHER GEAR

When it comes to sleeping bags, the most important piece of a tent camping sleep system, refer to the label for the temperature they are suited to – a three-season sleeping bag would suit summer camping in Europe or the USA but winters there, or in colder places, may demand a warmer one. Remember that temperatures often drop at night, sometimes by 20 degrees or more, so when choosing a sleeping bag, pay attention to the season and temperature rating to ensure it will keep you at the optimum temperature for the time of year you choose to camp.

There are generally two types of sleeping bag – down-filled or synthetic – so buy according to your budget and planned uses. A sleeping mat is a great item to have, as it offers valuable insulation between the body and the ground and contributes to a good night's sleep. This is important because even if you have an ultra-warm down sleeping bag, as sleeping on the down filling compresses it, making it less effective and not as warm. In areas where temperatures typically drop overnight, such as California, where night-time temperatures regularly drop below 40 degrees even in the middle of summer, you'll want something robust. Down sleeping bags are rated down to certain temperatures but are pricier than the inexpensive synthetic rectangular 'caravan' ones in most shops. While down bags offer the greatest warmth, synthetic filled ones are usually lighter and stay warmer when damp. Regardless of tent type, a decent sleeping bag can mean the difference between a comfortable, restful night's sleep and a wide-awake night of freezing misery.

A torch or lantern helps light the tent after dark, helping with night-time toilet trips and making finding things in your tent or in the 4x4 easier. Head torches score here as they leave both hands free.

Most campsites already have picnic tables scattered about, but for more remote camping you could carry a sturdy compact surface to prep and cook your food on – folding tables and chairs are the key here. A folding chair that's comfortable and quick to set up around the fire is a valuable luxury, and it is a bonus if it has a cup holder in one of its arms. Chairs around the fire lend themselves to sociable camping. Items like this make the difference between setting up a camp that you'll relax in for the weekend as opposed to a quick overnight place to crash, but remember there are times when either approach works.

It is worth getting some sort of box to contain the kitchen equipment, as it keeps it all together. Furthermore, its lid can act as worktop, and it can easily be lifted in and out of the 4x4. When considering its contents, remember that you can be realistic about whether you actually need expensive equipment. For example, cheap plastic plates and bowls work just fine and last for years. Cheap gas stoves also work well, so long as they have some sort of windshield.

Do some meal planning ahead of your trip, and stock up on the food you need. Knowing what you're going to eat and how you're going to cook it can save time and effort. Aim for a decent camp breakfast, simple lunch supplies you can prepare on the tailgate and plan evening meals or barbecues. One way to make things easy is to buy foods that only require one pan or only require water to make them edible rather than more complex preparation. Depending on local regulations, building a campfire and cooking dinner over an open flame can be the perfect end to a great day outdoors.

Larger tents offer somewhere to cook on rainy days, and items such as folding tables make such tasks easier.

The reality of camping off the beaten track in Morocco; dome tents on a flat but hard-surfaced campsite in the metaphorical middle of nowhere.

Camping in the snow in dome tents is not much different, except for being much colder.

With a 4x4, it is easy to camp in comfort too; folding tables and chairs, boxes for the food and kitchen items, camp beds and sleeping bags in an awning tent all make a stay luxurious.

A compromise between surviving and a luxurious campsite is a small convenient dome tent, folding table and chairs and a smaller amount of cooking equipment that can be easily carried in a 4x4.

# WATER

Water is essential for survival in the great outdoors, and the further off the beaten path you go, the more important it becomes. The last thing anyone needs is to be stuck without a supply of fresh running water, especially as drinking from a river, pond or lake can cause serious illness due to bacteria.

## WATER FILTRATION

Clean water is something a lot of people take for granted, but you may be without clean water in the wilderness. Even if you're car camping at a managed campsite with a potable water pump, I recommend having a backup on hand, just in case. Packing a filter of some sort, such as a canvas Millbank bag, and water purification tablets in your camping box will mean any source of water can be yours for drinking.

Pictured is a personal water filter that relies on gravity to let water flow through three filters, one made from sponge to catch grit and sand and two smaller gauze filets of different size gauze. The filter kit is designed to fit the wide mouth of military-type water bottles and when not in use, all its components nest together to make it a compact unit to carry.

Various types of filters are available and most work on the principle of letting the water run through the filter, which can be ceramic or metal gauze, into a container where puritabs can be added or the water decanted for boiling prior to drinking. The tried and tested range of ceramic Katadyn filters from Switzerland are designed to remove bacteria, protozoa and other disease-causing agents. These microorganisms cannot be pumped through the pores of the ceramic filter because their size is greater than 0.2 microns. Unlike similar equipment with disposable filters, the ceramic filter can be cleaned numerous times, and this makes it suitable for the toughest of conditions so, for decades, military and emergency professionals around the world have used the Katadyn filters.

On the 1991 Camel Trophy, in a particularly wet and overgrown section of the route, much of the event convoy was resorting to winching through one muddy obstacle after another, making slow progress. The humidity meant that everyone was thirsty, so drinking water and water for tea was in demand. During the spells of waiting, we resorted to filtering the water gathered out of the ruts behind the Land Rover Discovery. We had a small Katadyn water filter and started by filtering water so muddy that the filter blocked after only a few strokes of the pump. Subsequently someone's t-shirt was sacrificed to be used as a filter to catch the worst of the mud and then this water was passed through the Katadyn filter before being decanted into the Kelly Kettle for vigorous boiling to kill the microorganisms and then turned into very welcome cups of tea before we winched though the next obstacle.

## TOILETS

Hardcore wilderness campers may view toilet paper as an unnecessary luxury, but many consider it a necessity for comfort and hygiene. If you're camping in the woods and concerned about the environmental impact of using toilet paper, purchase some that's biodegradable or take a refuse bag for disposal. You can carry a waste disposal system comprising a trowel, hand wash and toilet paper when wild camping and bury your waste. For shower necessities, repackaging ordinary bathroom products in smaller containers before a trip can be worthwhile.

# FIRE

Some feel that camping isn't camping without a warm, crackling campfire, or 'bush TV' as it is referred to in Australia and Africa, so you'll want the tools to get one started quickly. Campers can start fires with a flint and steel, matches, a cigarette lighter or a magnesium fire starter. If you opt for matches, make sure they are waterproof or in a sealed container. It's not a bad idea to pack two fire starters in case one fails. Take along a little kindling as well, such as dry bark or thin twigs, in a waterproof container. Dry birch bark burns particularly well. Remember that finding dry kindling outdoors when you need it can be a challenge depending on weather (see Camp and Cooking Fires, p. 201).

The golden rule is that, when it's time to strike camp and pack up to move on, make sure you leave no trace, so it looks as though you were never there.

## CAMPING CHECKLISTS

A recommended list of camping essentials to take on any trip.

### Camping gear – preparation is the key

- Tent or tents (to accommodate the entire group)
- Sleeping bag (one for each member of the group)
- Sleeping mat or camp bed if tent camping (one for each member of the group)
- Kitchen equipment including camping stove and the correct type of fuel; kettle; cooking pans and utensils/cutlery; tin and bottle opener, found on tools such as a Swiss Army knife; lighter/matches
- Water carrier or jerrycan (especially if camping away from a water source)
- Trowel and poo bags for burying or removing toilet waste
- Rubbish bags (if you pack it in, pack it out)

## Camp luxuries – there's no need to be uncomfortable!

- Pillow(s)
- A cool box or 12v plug-in fridge
- Washing-up bowl and liquid
- Folding table
- Camping chair(s)
- Windbreak
- Lantern for lighting the tent/being able to cook in the evening
- Air pump, if required for an airbed
- Rubber mallet for knocking in tent pegs

## Personal gear – stay warm and weatherproof

- Waterproof jacket and trousers
- Suitable footwear
- Woolly hat and/or sunhat
- Gloves
- Suitable footwear
- Clean and dry spare clothes and underwear
- Spare underwear and socks
- Torch or head torch

## Health and safety – stay clean and healthy

- Sun protection and sunglasses
- Toiletries, including soap and shampoo
- Towel
- Any prescribed medicines
- First aid kit
- Hand sanitiser and antibacterial wipes
- Insect repellent
- Toothbrush and toothpaste
- Toilet paper

# WILD CAMPING EQUIPMENT

To go wild camping, you need to be able to use a map and compass and know what to wear and carry for safety in the great outdoors. Many see the minimum as a tent, sleeping bag, sleeping mat and a lightweight single-burner stove, gas canister and lighter, pot, spork (the useful all-in-one fork and spoon) and mug for a hot drink. Wild campers might choose to eat a one-pot meal from the pot or put their meal in the mug, which they can also use for coffee or tea. Dehydrated camping food is one option, as it only requires water for cooking. Water is another essential, but if the campsite is near running water, less water needs carrying. Boil collected water for cleanliness or carry water purification tablets. The absolute basics for cooking could be a Kelly Kettle, a mug, a spork and some dehydrated noodles.

## WILD CAMPING TIPS

- Camp discreetly.
- Pitch late and strike camp early.
- Take care not to damage vegetation, especially at altitudes above the tree line where it can be susceptible to trampling.
- Do not light fires on peaty soils and dry grass because of the risk of the fire spreading.
- Do not pollute water courses in any way.
- If it is not possible to take toilet waste away, make sure it is buried at least 15cm below ground and covered.
- Do not bury used toilet paper.
- Remove all food and waste that might attract scavengers or put animals at risk.
- Carry all waste away when you leave.

# IMPROVISED SHELTERS

If, for any reason, tents or other forms of shelter are not available, there may be a need for improvised shelter. During the summer, the only protection required may be from insects, but in colder seasons a shelter that offers some warmth will be more crucial. In winter, it is not possible to stay out in the open for long without the exertion of moving to keep warm, so improvised shelters need to be constructed. What can be built depends on what is available, and that depends on the terrain. In open terrain, a shelter can be built using canvas sheets or snow blocks. Snow caves, snow holes or even igloos can be built in winter conditions. In temperate woodland, a lean-to shelter or bivouac can be made from branches and fallen wood, but comfort depends on a degree of initiative and improvisation. A lean-to can be made by putting a fallen branch between two trees or against one and covering the windward side of this rudimentary frame with a basha sheet, overlapping fallen branches to create an angled wall that offers a degree of insulation and can be used to sit or lie behind. If suitable trees are not available to create the frame, A-frames can be made from shorter pieces of wood. An open fire can be used to heat such a shelter, but take care not to burn the shelter – or the forest – down. Snow caves can be excavated with a shovel in deep and compacted snow wherever it drifts, including riverbanks, cliffs and in the lee of ridges. Improvisation is key here, but make the cave high enough to sit in comfortably and find some insulation to sit or lie on. A sleeping mat can be bolstered with cardboard from a food box, for example.

Basha sheets are useful for improvised shelters. Suspended from trees or roof racks, they can act as a shelter while cooking or, nearer the ground, they can provide a rainproof shelter to sleep under.

This small basha sheet has been rigged on the side of a Land Rover to offer a degree of shade from the sun, something that can be useful in hot destinations.

Large groups can be easily accommodated in dome tents, but often it is more fun to travel in small groups and enjoy camping from a 4x4 off the beaten track.

# EATING AND DRINKING

## CAMP COOKING

Part of an Irish blessing wishes 'a roof for the rain, a warm cup of tea by the fire and laughter to cheer you'. All these things contribute to great camping experiences. Remember, if you're tired or hungry, your camping experience will be memorable for the wrong reasons.

A 4x4 can take you to some interesting places to prepare a meal.

# KELLY KETTLE

Kelly Kettle is actually a brand name for a type of chimney kettle that has been made in County Mayo in the Republic of Ireland since the 1900s. Other names for similar devices are 'storm kettle', 'ghillie kettle' and 'volcano kettle', while the New Zealanders in the desert war of World War Two referred to them as 'Benghazi burners'. Author Alice Walker said, 'Tea to the English is really a picnic indoors', but with this device you can have tea and a picnic out of doors.

There were once plans for making one from soldered food tins in a vintage Boy's Own-type how-to manual, and there are also numerous other trademarked names; George Marris & Co of Birmingham produced the Sirram Volcano Kettle in England in the 1920s and the Thermette was first manufactured in New Zealand during the 1930s. More recent trade names include Eydon, Ghillie and Eco Trekker, all are portable devices for boiling water outdoors.

The ingenious Kelly Kettles have been made in County Mayo in the west of Ireland for more than a century.

The Eco Trekker is another proprietary brand of the chimney kettle that relies on the heat warming the water in the outer jacket of the flue.

Made from stainless steel or aluminium, these kettles comprise a water jacket surrounding a fire chimney that draws heat from the tiny fire in the bottom across a large surface area, thus ensuring a very rapid boiling of the water in all conditions. This means that the Kelly Kettle can boil water outdoors in a few minutes by burning a small handful of tiny sticks, pine cones, bark or even dry grass. The key to the speed is using dry fuel, and during my introduction to the Kelly Kettle it was this that was often in short supply.

It was during the 1991 Tanzania-Burundi Camel Trophy that I first became aware of the Kelly Kettle; the convoy was moving slowly in the often boggy, wet and humid conditions, so drinks were crucial in keeping people sweating over winch cables and vehicle recoveries going. In the GB team Discovery, we had plenty of tea and dried milk, we had a water purifier pump for cleaning water from ruts, so all we needed was hot water. In the wet sections, there was no dry wood, but we had plenty of diesel in jerrycans and I discovered that, with a tissue to act as a wick in a drop

*Above*: An indication of the small sized pieces of stick that will bring water to the boil in a chimney kettle in just a few minutes.

*Opposite*: A Kelly Kettle being used with diesel fuel during the wet conditions of the 1991 Camel Trophy in Tanzania and Burundi.

of diesel, the water boiled quickly. As vehicles and teams worked their way through obstacles, there was plenty of time to get the large Kelly on; I remember my mum's admonishment at us boiling the water vigorously and making tea while waiting for our vehicle's turn to cross the obstacle or waiting for others behind us and swigging it in between helping. Tea with powdered milk and a hint of diesel, lovely... People drank it as fast as I could make it, though. That said, these days, woodsmoke and semi-skimmed milk is preferable.

Kelly Kettles and other similar types became popular with 4x4 enthusiasts but are also used by fishermen, who often point out that the smoke from the chimney helps keep riverbank midges at bay and canoe travellers say similar. The smaller ones are becoming popular

The one-pint (600ml) capacity Kelly ‘Trekker’ provides ample capacity for one or two people.

with backpackers, because they do not require fuel to be carried, and the one-pint (600ml) anodised aluminium model, now known as a Kelly 'Trekker', is ideal for two people who are travelling light, because of its lightness of weight and small size.

## TRANGIA

The Swedish Trangia company was founded in 1925 by John E. Jonsson. John and his father-in-law started a company manufacturing household pots in aluminium. However, as camping holidays increased in popularity with Swedish workers in the 1930s, the demand for camping equipment grew and Trangia decided to develop cooking products specifically for camping. By 1951, the first prototype of the Trangia stove system was developed and launched. The concept was a compact and complete cooking system burning

The windproof Trangia stove is a compact coking system that packs the meths burner, kettle and pans into one easily carried package

methylated spirits, liquid fuel, an efficient fuel that was easy to use. The name Trangia is derived from the village of Trång. Since then, the product has been one of the outdoor market's strongest brands worldwide. It is still manufactured in Sweden, in the same village where John E. Jonsson started his business.

## HEXAMINE STOVE

The hexamine stove, or 'hexy-burner', is a military cooking stove that uses hexamine fuel tablets – officially hexamethyl-enetetramine or methenamine. The stove acts as a platform for the cooking vessel and a partial windbreak for such cooking. The windbreak part of the stove is designed to fold into a compact size that can be used to contain the fuel tablets. The hexy burner has long been used by the British Army, in conjunction with mess tins and compo rations.

The hexamine stove is a simple folding stove that burns fuel tablets and heats water quickly.

Time caught up with the hexy stove, and it has now been replaced with a more modern eco-friendly stove from BCB International that uses ethanol-based 'Fire Dragon' fuel. The Ministry of Defence requirement for the new stove was for it to boil half a litre of water in under 11 minutes.

## CAMPINGAZ

Campingaz, pronounced as 'camping gas', was formerly Camping Gaz, a brand of compressed, mixed butane/propane gas supplied in distinctive blue, disposable cylinders as a fuel for a range of appliances, specifically manufactured for camp cookers, lanterns, heaters and grills. The company was founded in France in 1949 and rapidly expanded to foreign markets so that its blue products were an unmistakable part of many campers' equipment. In 1996, Camping Gaz became part of Coleman Inc., now part of the Jarden Corporation, and its brand name was modernised to Campingaz in 1998.

Campingaz stoves and lamps rely on canisters of mixed propane and butane and were hugely popular with campers for many years. This is still a cheap way to cook when camping with a 4x4.

The disposable Gaz cartridges are made from thin metal, and inserting one into the cooker pierces it, then, once the appliance's valve is opened, it enables the gas to flow. There is also now a range of self-sealing valve-type cartridges, which can be disconnected and reconnected at will for storage or transport. The company also produces a range of larger refillable butane cylinders for larger multi-burner camp stoves.

## CADAC GRILL

This type of handy little stove can be very useful when you're out and about. Though not suitable for, nor designed for, backpackers, it's reasonably lightweight at 1.5kg, and it folds neatly into its own carry case so won't take up much space in the back of a 4x4. Made by Cadac, a trusted brand from South Africa, the robust Cook & Grill 230 is perfect for a spontaneous brew up or BBQ in the great outdoors because of its

Cadac camping stoves and grills are made in South Africa and enable a braai (a South African BBQ) to be both portable and gas fuelled.

versatility. Fuelled by standard threaded gas cartridges, it is powerful enough to boil a litre of water in less than five minutes, and it can take pans or pots up to 30cm in diameter. It also incorporates a non-stick reversible grill plate that enables a variety of different foods to be grilled or fried.

## PRESSURE STOVES

The paraffin (kerosene) pressure stove first appeared in the 19th century, when Frans Wilhelm Lindqvist, patented his 'Sootless Kerosene Stove'. His design was successful, and, together with partner J. V. Svensson, a company was formed to manufacture the stove and named 'Primus', Latin for 'first'. Later, Roald Amundsen used a Primus during his quest to be first to reach thc South Pole, and, in 1953, Edmund Hillary used Primus stoves on the first successful Mount Everest expedition, so the name became the generic one used by many people to describe any pressurised camp stove. The design burns paraffin gas, which is vapourised from the liquid fuel in the tubes that form the burner head.

Optimus was founded in Stockholm in 1899, and, in a quirk of fate, in 1962, the paraffin division of Primus was sold to Optimus. Despite this, it continued to manufacture stoves under the name Primus until 1972, when the range was consolidated to just Optimus models, which continued in production until 1996 when the range was superseded by petrol and multi-fuel stoves. The No 7 stove was a petrol version of the pressure stove produced for the British Army and one of a range of numbered stoves that were used from the 1950s to the 1970s and made by companies such as Optimus and Valor. The portable Optimus is a slightly different design from the, arguably better-known, Primus, but essentially, both types work the same way. The tubes are heated with a drop of methylated spirit, burned in the circular tray, and, with the initial pressure provided by a small hand-operated pump integrated into the stove's brass tank, the paraffin vapour comes out of a jet and burns. The heat is deflected by a spreader ring, and it burns so hot that the flame is barely visible but very audible, to the extent that some refer to these

The pressure stove originated in Scandinavia and burns paraffin (kerosene). Various sizes were offered, including those that dismantle for transport.

Those on the 1955 First Overland Land Rover expedition from London to Singapore used pressure stoves to cook their food.

stoves as 'roarers'. The flame on such a stove is adjusted by using the pump to increase the pressure in the tank to make the flame larger and hotter, or by venting the tank with the knurled pressure release to lower pressure and so reduce the flame.

Depending on where you are travelling, you may not need to bring absolutely everything, as many car camping-friendly campsites are equipped with a fire-pit and a grate to cook on, as well as picnic tables for food prep and eating. More remote and wild campsites will have no such facilities, and this is when the fold-down tailgate of many 4x4s comes into its own as a working surface and table. Most campsites in bear country also include a bear box (but you may also need to bring along a bear canister).

# KITCHEN UTENSILS

## WATER BOTTLE

There's nothing more irritating than having to hike to the water tap every time you need water, so take a water bottle or canteen. Remember that, in

There is no shortage of water bottles available from sports and outdoor shops and all suit cooking on the tailgate of a 4x4.

very cold weather, a plastic item will freeze, especially if left outside a tent overnight, and plastic bottles cannot be thawed over a flame. Water can be stopped from freezing by keeping the water bottle in a sleeping bag with a sleeper overnight. Some canteens have a mug that fits over them, providing a compact way to transport both items.

## CAN OPENER

While many pocketknives have a can opener as one of the folding tools, the army-type pocket can opener is a useful tool for expeditions. The US Army version was designed by the Subsistence Research Laboratory of the US Army in Chicago and subsequently made in two sizes, the P-38 and the larger P-51. The smaller one is just 38mm in length, suggesting the origin of its description is its size, and, not surprisingly, the P-51 is 51mm in size. They originated in 1942 and were made in the US by the Shelby Co., and were part of the military issue ration pack. British ones were made by Morfed.

They have a little hole for a lanyard or keyring, and the flat edge at the end can be used as an emergency screwdriver. The cutter is hinged, so it can be stored in next to no space and folds out again for use. The notch is used to grip the rim of a can, it is then levered around the top using the fold out cutter to make slits in the lid. Cut enough slits and the tin top can be bent open. Different versions were made; for example, the Australians added a spoon-shaped end for eating.

## DRINKING MUG

A cup of hot tea or coffee while watching the sunrise is an unmissable camping experience, so bring a mug or thermos to put that drink in. There's plastic, titanium and enamel mugs, and all have advantages, but many prefer metal mugs as they can be heated directly over the fire on a grate or kept warm on a hot rock next to the fire.

# MESS KIT

Disposable paper plates may seem like an environmentally friendly option, but reusable plates and bowls are even more eco-friendly and will save waste for years to come. There's also something comforting about getting a favourite camping mug out of your kit for that special camping cuppa. It's the same story with utensils; disposable plastic cutlery is banned in many places, and reusable items are more environmentally friendly. Any old cutlery will suffice, but a spork will usually work, and a folding version can be carried inside a mug.

With pans, think about scale, as you do not need huge pans if you are only cooking for two. You won't need many if you are cooking simple things or heating and rehydrating dehydrated food. There is an endless selection of camping pans available, and they are often referred to as 'Billies' and 'Dixies'. Nesting ones with folding handles are easier to pack and many –

The US Army mess kit is convenient because its two components nest together and the handle folds in so that it is compact.

UK military mess tins also nest and have folding handles, and the empty pans can be used to carry food and utensils when not in use.

A traditional cast iron skillet is suited to cooking on embers, because this kind of pan heats evenly when a fire varies in temperature.

The base of a chimney cooker such as a Kelly Kettle or Eco Trekker (here) can be used to cook with a small pan.

especially military types – can be used to heat the food and then as a plate to eat it off. A traditional favourite for cooking over the fire is a cast iron skillet because not every frying pan can handle cooking on an open fire. Plastic handles, for example, may melt over the fire, and cast iron is the ideal material for a frying pan because it will evenly distribute heat, which is important when cooking over open flames since the heat source may be spread out or variable.

## CUTTING BOARD

Depending on what is to be cooked, a small chopping board and a kitchen knife don't take up much room in a kitchen box and are easier to use than a Swiss Army knife when preparing vegetables.

## SKEWERS

Some don't think a camping trip is complete without cooking over the fire with skewers. Reusable BBQ skewers are readily available and offer an alternative to burning a hand using chopsticks or scavenged twigs. Instead of impaling sausages, it is easy to bend up a wire holder from fence wire to grip several sausages firmly and cook them without dropping them into the fire. With two or three of these holders, enough for a large group can be grilled.

## FRIDGE OR COOLER

This is getting into luxury camping territory, but it's a way to keep perishable food and beer cold. There are plenty of plug-in versions of an electric fridge available, just be careful not to flatten your 4x4's battery overnight.

# FOOD

This might seem obvious, but keep in mind how many calories you'll need for strenuous activities such as swimming, hiking or winching your 4x4. Create a basic meal plan before leaving and take all the ingredients it will need. Most of what we eat and drink is used in maintaining our body heat, while only a small portion is used in producing energy for physical work. Ensure adequate calorific intake especially in cold-weather operations. About 4,000 calories per day is necessary for people performing demanding work in the cold. Efficiency may drop rapidly if this level is not maintained.

## MILITARY RATIONS

Military rations provide the needed calories for soldiers to live and fight effectively, and much can be learned from this. When eaten in their entirety, ration packs contain the right amount of carbohydrates, fats,

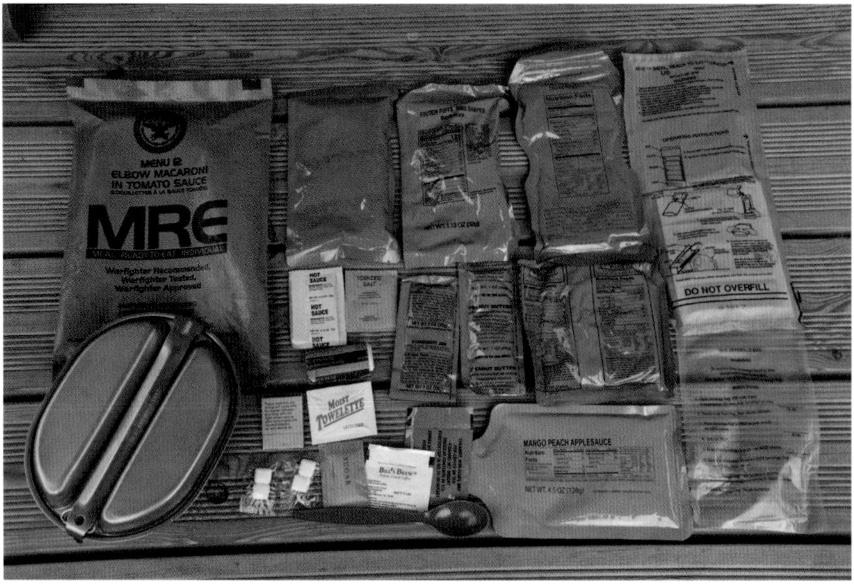


The US 24-hour ration pack includes MREs (Meals Ready to Eat) and everything else a soldier needs to operate for 24 hours, all in a sealed plastic packet.

The British Army ration pack contains similar rations and adequate calories for 24 hours in breakfast, main meals, drinks and snacks portions.

With careful shopping in supermarkets, it is possible to emulate MREs to provide sufficient calories for strenuous activity in portable and convenient packages.

Competitors in the selection event for the 2006 Land Rover G4 Challenge event eat convenient meals that only require the addition of hot water.

protein and vitamins. American, British and other nations' ration packs are different in appearance but are all designed to serve the same purpose of providing the right amount of nutrition. However, the proper intake of these essential items depends on the entire ration being eaten in properly spaced intervals. Any lack of concern regarding eating caused by the cold, combined with the difficulties and inconvenience of cooking, may tempt people to miss meals. The principles of sound leadership and discipline in cold weather require that meals be prepared, and that the entire ration be warmed and eaten when possible. The included snacks should be saved for between meals and when moving. It is possible to emulate military-style rations with regular supermarket items, although care should be taken to purchase foods that only require water to be added, for simplicity and convenience.

### SPICES AND CONDIMENTS

Nothing ruins a good meal more than a lack of seasoning or condiments, even on something as basic as hot dogs. Regular campers often take essentials in a camping box; a supply of salt, pepper, Italian seasoning, curry paste, cooking oil or ketchup carried in small waterproof containers. This is a trick worth copying.

## TRAVELLING LIGHT

Although making tea and coffee drinks with a Kelly Kettle is obvious, with careful shopping it is possible to buy numerous packet foods that only need hot water adding before eating. Examples are porridge and dried noodles, so, if there's water and sticks where you're going, it is possible to eat well with little more kitchen equipment than a Kelly Kettle, a mug and a spork. Even in wet forests, it's usually possible to find dry, small sticks of the size needed to fit in the base of the stove on the ground around the bottom of trees. Just don't forget the matches and take every care not to burn your tent or the forest down.

If there's water and bits of stick where you're going, you can travel light with nothing more than a one-pint Kelly Kettle, matches, a mug and spork and a selection of packet foods and drinks. The length of a trip determines how many packets will be required.

Sometimes though, food on 4x4 trips, such as here in Spain, can be even simpler!

The Eco Trekker enables water to boiled very quickly almost anywhere, meaning that hot food or a hot drink is never far away.

The base of the Eco Trekker can also be used for social tasks, such a toasting marshmallows over its flames.

# CAMP AND COOKING FIRES

On 4x4 trips that involve overnighting, a campfire will act as a focal point during the hours of darkness, entertaining campers with its dancing flames. Many believe that a camping trip is not complete until an evening has been spent relaxing with friends around the fire; chat and banter, beers and grilled food or roasted marshmallows under an open sky make for a great night. The campfire undoubtedly helps create a peaceful atmosphere, and also has the benefit of providing warmth and heat for cooking. With a little bit of knowledge and practice, it is possible to adjust a fire to do either the former or the latter. With a cooking fire, it is best to cook on embers rather than flames and small logs of dead wood burn to embers quickly but may need replenishing when used for cooking over an extended period.

## CAMPFIRES

In many areas, campfires are restricted, so make sure you abide by the rules. The golden rule is to keep fires small, under control and supervised at all times to avoid the risk of wildfires and damage to the local area. Ground fires are often surrounded by a circle of stones, and reusing the same spot minimises damage. Increasingly, protecting the ground from heat is becoming important, so metal barbecues, fire baskets, fire pits and

An evening campsite fire during an overland 4x4 trip to Morocco.

The warmth and spectacle of a campfire adds to the ambience of any night camping in the great outdoors.

A circle of stones on the ground contains a campfire and allows the same spot to be reused, avoiding increasing damage to the ground.

raised fires that are a lot more environmentally friendly than campfires are becoming popular. In a 4x4, it is possible to carry such devices.

Using stones for a kettle or pan support seems the handiest options sometimes, but the heat can crack one or more of the stones and tip the kettle over or land the sausages in the ashes. A fire pit is an open, lidless container in which a wood fire can be lit. Fire pits are raised above the ground on legs, meaning you won't leave any burned grass or ground below the fire. It can be cooked over or just lit for the warmth. If cooking, it can be used in conjunction with a traditional, lightweight camping stove. A fire pan is a metal plate raised 3–5in above the floor on which the fire burns. Place stones under each of its corners to raise it above the ground. If you are wild camping, leave no trace of the fire. One way to do this it to carefully dig up a patch of grass, then replace it to hide the cold ashes.

Gather wood responsibly (dead wood, this is relatively light when picked up and breaks by hand) or buy firewood from a local source. This helps to protect the surrounding woodlands that are crucial to the local ecosystem. Burning freshly cut wood is often difficult because of its high moisture content. Whatever fuel you opt for, it needs to be dry to burn well and reduce smoke.

There is a huge variety of fire baskets available, and many are small enough to transport in a 4x4. The advantage such fire baskets offer is that they keep the fire off the ground, avoiding damage to grass and plants.

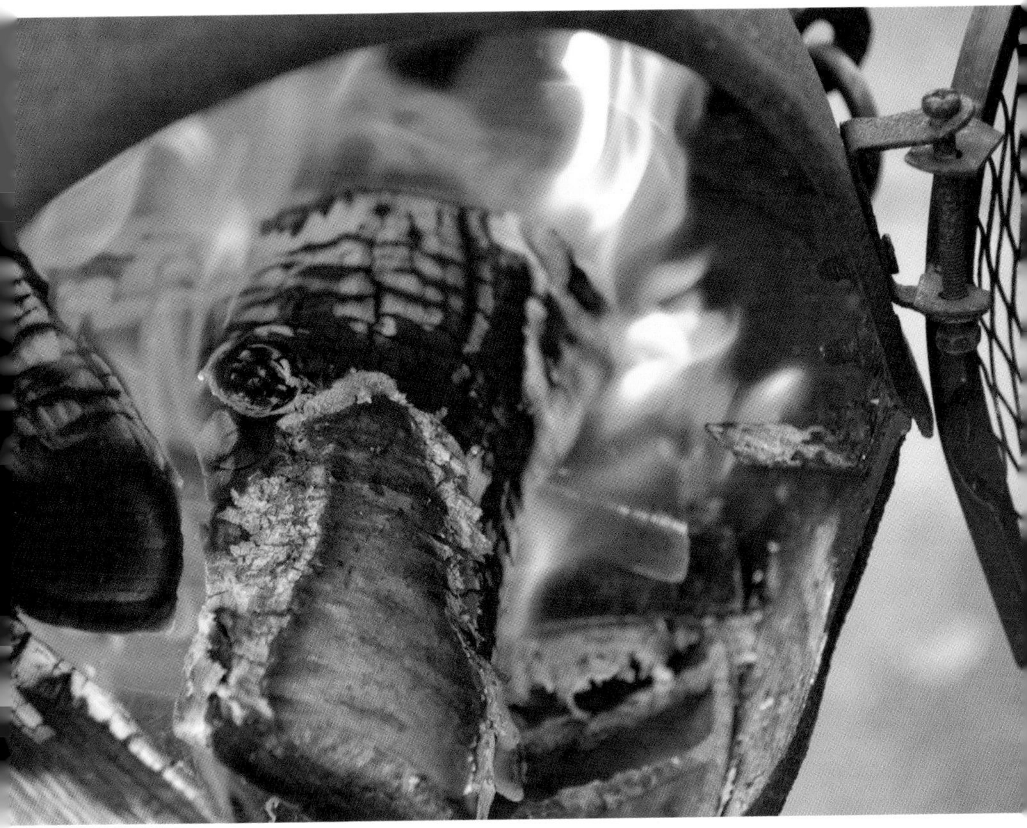

For a campfire, collect dead wood that has dried out. This will light easily and burn well while keeping smoke to a minimum.

Build the fire in a spot away from overhanging branches, dry grass or anything that may enable it to spread. Gather some tinder, small pieces of dry leaves, grass, tiny twigs and bits of newspaper. Form these into a neat pile, then gather some bigger, dry twigs and position them over the tinder in a teepee shape. Light the tinder in a couple of places, and the teepee will let oxygen reach the twigs as the flames are drawn through it. As the flames take hold, add small sticks of kindling to the fire. Then progressively add bigger sticks to the fire until it is big enough to burn logs. Once the logs are burning, crack a beer and life is good. The main thing to remember to take with you is matches or a lighter!

To get the fire going, light the kindling then add bigger dry sticks, and once these are ablaze add bigger logs.

Keep the fire small enough to put out quickly if necessary, and if possible, keep water, sand or earth on hand to extinguish it. Or, of course, there is the old standby of urine, but do be careful!

## COOKING FIRES

There are numerous methods and techniques for cooking on a campfire, but it is not possible to recommend any as the 'best', as the type of camping trip, type of food, type of fuel and even the surrounding terrain dictate the method that is best on that occasion. Where weight and space are not an issue such as when 4x4 camping, the use of a grill is one of the best cooking methods. It is easily and quickly set up, a variety of food can be cooked on it and, because it offers a flat surface, it is ideal for balancing pans and a kettle.

Once the cooking fire is going, let it burn down until there are few big flames. Like a barbecue, cook over hot embers, so once it has reduced a little, rake the embers to even them out and begin cooking. It is possible to rake some hot embers to the side, while keeping the main fire going to supply further cooking embers as required.

When clearing up and preparing to leave, remember: if it's too hot to touch, it's too hot to leave. Douse a fire thoroughly with water, check for any still smouldering embers and finally double check that it is extinguished. Wildfires can be an environmental disaster.

Some sort of basket contains a cooking fire and offers a place for a grille to put the pans and kettle on over the heat. Start with small sticks and logs that will turn into embers quickly and be prepared to add more sticks as the fire smoulders.

It is common to cook on the embers of a larger campfire and the same principle applies, burn some small sticks and logs in order to create embers to cook on.

Almost any kind of metal grille can be used to cook on. As an example, this is the wire radiator grille from a Land Rover being used over a fire (care should be taken here not to inhale fumes from the zinc galvanising).

Small portable cookers that are fuelled with wood are available. This one folds out from flat into a cooker suitable for one pan or kettle. It is small but cooks in the same way as larger fires.

No matter your means of transport, a campfire and a basic tent enable you to experience the great outdoors.

A mug of tea or coffee by a remote campfire is a quiet moment to be savoured.

# TOOLS AND REPAIRS

When it comes to off-road repairs and trail fixes, it is worth remembering that prevention is always better than cure. In many cases, damage off-road is incurred by careless or over-exuberant driving. Therefore, driving with care and mechanical sympathy will eliminate many potential breakdowns, and that is considerably better than fixing a 4x4.

To further eliminate problems, leave home with a properly serviced vehicle, and, with any luck, this will guarantee an uneventful off-road trip. Regardless of the type of terrain your 4x4 vehicle is used in, there are basic maintenance necessities.

All 4x4 vehicles need regular oil and filter changes, coolant checks, new air filters, lubrication of wheel bearings and propshaft UJs and regular servicing to keep them running reliably. Remember, the jobs may need doing more often than the manufacturer recommends if your

## TOOL KIT ESSENTIALS

- Adjustable spanner
- Allen keys
- Ball pein hammer
- Cable ties
- Electrical and duct tape
- Jump leads
- Mole/vice grips
- Multimeter
- Oil rags
- Pliers and wire cutters
- Pocket knife
- Slot and Phillips screwdrivers
- Socket set (metric or imperial, depending on vehicle)
- Spare rope/rachet straps
- Super glue
- Tyre pressure gauge
- Vehicle jack
- WD-40
- Work gloves

## SPARES ESSENTIALS

- Coolant or water
- Engine oil
- Funnel and siphon hose
- Fuses of all types fitted in your 4x4
- Gaskets
- Heater and coolant hoses (or a length of universal hose)
- Hose clamps (various sizes)
- Length of wire
- Oil and air filters
- Power steering or transmission fluid
- Radiator stop leak
- Selection of nuts and bolts
- Solder and soldering iron
- Spare bulbs for all lights
- Spare tyres, tyre repair kit, inner tube and tyre changing tools
- Spark plugs, points, coil for petrol engines

4x4 is used in extreme conditions such as deep mud, heavy dust or sandy desert environments. Off-road travel and rocky road-induced vibrations can also loosen bolts and suspension components.

General maintenance also includes checking that lights, wipers, and accessories are working properly. Suspension components – especially

Overland travel may involve working on vehicles in less than 'workshop' conditions. Here, a Jeep is serviced in Egypt's Western Desert. Tools are stood upright in the sand to avoid them becoming lost.

aftermarket suspension – should be regularly greased as required, as this increases longevity and performance. Related to this, perform regular suspension and shock absorber checks including re-torquing nuts and bolts. Fully torqued components can be marked with a paint marker to provide a quick 'at a glance' check to see if anything has loosened off before it becomes a problem.

Modern 4x4s will have a warning light on the dashboard to remind about rotating tyres to ensure even wear. Something else that ensures even wear is properly inflated tyres at the recommended pressures for road driving. Airing down for off-road use means that they have to be reinflated at some point. The air pressure to drop to depends on a 4x4's tyre size, weight and the terrain. Replace worn tyres before heading off-road, as the loss of traction from worn treads might leave you stuck in muddy sections of a trail.

The range of tools, recovery and winching kit and all-important Kelly Kettle carried by Camel Trophy vehicles for their demanding journeys.

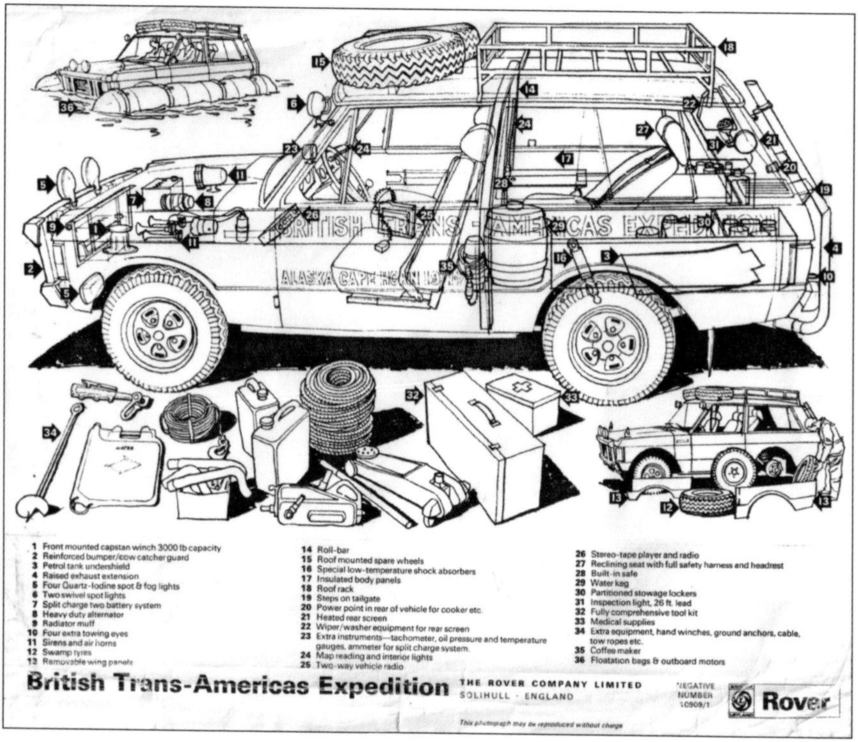


This diagram shows how all the tools and equipment were stowed in a Range Rover for the 1971 British Trans-Americas Expedition. Included are first aid and tool kits and a trolley jack, as well as a coffee maker. In the event itself, only the flotation devices were not carried.

This German-registered Toyota Land Cruiser carries its sand ladders on brackets on the vehicle's side from where they can be conveniently reached when required.

# TRAILSIDE REPAIRS

Even with proper maintenance and planning, breakdowns and problems can occur, and the key here is to be prepared when disaster strikes. There are lots of great stories of 'field fixes', such as splinting a broken leaf spring with two logs and some ratchet straps, using a plastic water carrier as a substitute for a radiator with a stick through it and welding with a series of batteries joined together with jump leads, but these are usually carried out by experienced off-roaders out of necessity.

The best solution is to take along some essentials and the tools to use them to enable temporary trail fixes to be made. Such repairs should be considered as a way to get back to the tarmac or make the drive home. Take parts and tools that you can use, but, even if you are experienced, you might not have the needed spare part or proper tool with you. Depending on the difficulty or length of your trip, carry radiator and heater hoses, drive belts, hose clamps, hardware and spare parts such as ignition components. It is also a good idea to have containers of coolant and oil in case something goes wrong.

A tool kit for trailside repairs should include basic tools and any other tools specific to your vehicle. A battery power pack capable of jump-starting your dead battery can also charge your phone. A tyre plug kit, inner tube and extra valves can be included, but a full-sized spare is always best.

Carrying a few spares and being prepared to think outside the box and improvise can really help when you are a long way from tarmac. Improvising means using different tools and items to sort out a problem out on the trails when the correct tools or replacement parts are not available. To do this, pack a small toolbox with cable ties, nuts, bolts, bits of plastic, radiator sealant, bits of rubber and anything else that could be useful. Remember, a spare bolt or nut can save a trip from failure.

The great stories about ingenious field fixes always form part of the campfire conversation and are more fun on subsequent trips! For example, when, miles from anywhere, a rubber oil hose split on a Land Rover I was driving, I had to work out a fix. Duct tape was a given, but I was concerned

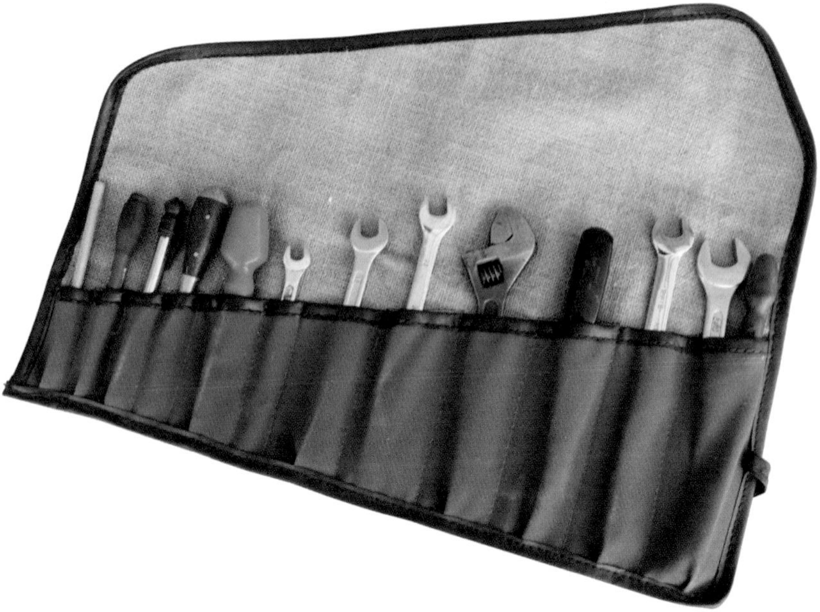

Carry a selection of tools that enable you to carry out any jobs you may have to do, including servicing and ignition repairs. A tool roll keeps them together and compact.

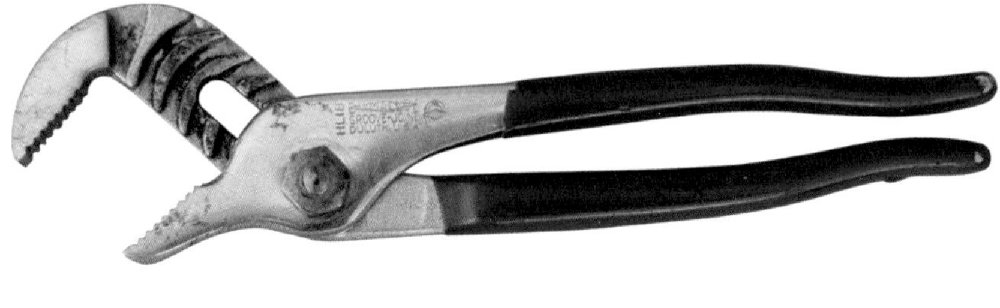

Tools such as these tongue and groove grips are useful for 4x4 trips because their adjustable nature means that they are suited to many jobs and sizes of nut and bolt.

that, when running, the engine's oil pressure would force the tape off the split. To prevent this, I put cable ties around the pipe and tape at 5mm intervals to hold the tape in place against the pressure. This repair lasted for almost two weeks until I arrived home.

## ROCKET SCIENCE – DUCT TAPE AND WD-40

Moving stuff, building stuff, fixing stuff and keeping stuff working miles from home often involves a great deal of banter among the people in question. As a result, there is a mass of collected wisdom for these situations; 'if it moves, grease it, if it doesn't, paint it', 'duct tape and vice grips' and my favourite, 'if it moves and it shouldn't, use duct tape, but if it doesn't move and it should, use WD-40'. One of the most key facets of this flippant wisdom is that, allegedly, you don't actually need a toolbox because, with these items, it is possible to fix anything – even a spaceship – so this is actually 'rocket science'.

### DUCT TAPE

In 1970, duct tape was fundamental in bringing Apollo 13 back from space and the edge of disaster. It might be hard to believe that sticky fabric tape brought a spaceship and three guys home from space, but it did. There was plenty of speculation in the papers and on TV about 13 being an unlucky number when things started to go badly wrong for astronauts in Apollo 13. The square carbon dioxide filters in the Apollo 13 command module needed to be modified to fit circular filter housings in the lunar module, which was being used as a 'lifeboat' to get the team back after a fuel tank malfunction en route to the moon. On the ground, a team put the exact contents of the spaceship on the table and said, 'We have to make this fit that with this stuff' and set to work. They came up with what we would now describe as a 'bodge job', to solve the problem, using duct tape and other bits on board Apollo 13.

The ground crew then relayed instructions to the spacecraft crew so they could replicate the bodge. It worked, and the $CO_2$ filters started to work again, saving the lives of James A. Lovell, John L. Swigert and Fred W. Haise. Ed Smylie, who worked on adapting the filters, said later that '[he] knew the problem was solvable when it was confirmed that duct tape was on the spacecraft'. The papers quoted him as saying, 'One thing a Southern boy will never say is, "I don't think duct tape will fix it"'.

The idea of problem solving with the pile of stuff on the table soon became one of those management training exercises, and, depending where you are in the world and what you're doing, duct tape goes by loads of names including pressure sensitive tape, canoe tape, gaffer tape, tank tape, racers' tape, gun tape, 100mph tape, riggers' tape, Duck Tape, fabric tape, speed tape, Gorilla Tape, hurricane tape and, in Germany, panzerband.

Duct tape, as a garage item, has its roots in the early post-war years. It has a standard width of 1⅞in (48mm) and was originally developed in 1942 as a water-resistant sealing tape for military ammunition boxes. Duck Tape and Gorilla Tape are current brands of the useful sticky tape, and its numerous uses have earned it respect in popular culture.

When it comes to repairing things with duct tape, the only limits are the imagination and innovation required for unusual fixes.

## WD-40 OIL

Another item that has earned equal respect in popular culture is WD-40. It is widely used and revered and dates back to the 1950s. WD-40 is the brand name of a lubricating, penetrating oil and water displacing spray, one of many now available. During 1953, it was developed by Norm Larsen of San Diego, California. As the name of Larsen's company – the Rocket Chemical Company – suggests, it also has a connection to rocket science. It is said that Rocket Chemical Company was attempting to create a formula to prevent corrosion in nuclear missiles by displacing the standing water that causes it.

Reportedly, while working in a small lab in San Diego, the team arrived at a successful formula on their 40th attempt, so WD-40, Water Displacement, 40th formula, was born. It was initially used to protect the outer skin and thin-walled balloon tanks of the Atlas missile from rust and corrosion by aerospace contractor Convair. The product actually worked well, and the Rocket Chemical Company's founder experimented with putting WD-40 into aerosol cans. He realised that members of the public would find a use for the product at home. So, in 1958, aerosols of WD-40 made their first appearance on store shelves in San Diego. Sure enough, as well as being a multipurpose spray for mechanics, it was later found to have numerous household uses.

Owners of wet 4x4s will no doubt relate to the tricks used to get a wet engine started; a squirt on the spark plug leads and inside the distributor can work wonders. During 1968, kits containing WD-40 were sent to soldiers in Vietnam to help keep their M-16 rifles in working condition in often wet and humid conditions, and, in 1969, the company was renamed after its only product, becoming WD-40 Company Inc. Amazingly, the original and secret formula for WD-40 is still in use today.

If duct tape can get a spaceship back from space and WD-40 can take care of missile fuel tanks, both products will work fine on most of the components of a 4x4. This is especially true when duct tape and WD-40

Aerosols of WD-40, the water displacing lubricant, and rolls of duct tape are widely well regarded for their multiple uses in temporary repairs.

are backed up with other staples of the 'near enough engineering' school of thought's inventory: baling twine, fence wire, Mole grips, multi-tools, a Swiss Army knife and a ball pein hammer.

## POCKET KNIVES

Despite offering a glimpse of the great outdoors to thousands of kids, the Scout Movement has, over the years, been the target of numerous jokes, including those about scouts having penknives with implements for getting stones out of horses' hooves and even boy scouts out of horses' hooves. However, the truth of the matter is that a penknife, pocket knife and, more latterly, a multi-tool, is often really useful as soon as you get outside the front door for work or play.

Here is a selection of the knives that can prove invaluable for camping and 4x4 driving. It's not a complete set by any means, but some didn't warrant inclusion in a section about working knives.

Left to right: Royal Navy folding knife and marlinspike; utility folding knife with wooden handle; French-made Opinel folding knife with wooden handle; Gerber 625 locking knife with rubber handle; Herbertz lock knife with ornate brass handle ends; one of the smaller Swiss Army combination knives.

The British Royal Navy-issue knife, made by Rodgers of Sheffield, came in handy for dealing with soggy ropes and its marlinspike was useful for dealing with steel shackles that were stiff or had rusted because of frequent exposure to water. It's the marlinspike that justifies the knife's inclusion here, simply because recovering bogged 4x4s frequently involves shackles, which rust if the thread isn't given a dab of copper grease.

This utility knife is not pretty in any way, being just a utility tool with a cheap wooden handle that is kept in a toolbox for dirty jobs such as scraping off underseal, trimming rubber hoses and cutting things that really demand wire cutters and hacksaws! It sharpens up on the oilstone and holds an edge well enough.

The Opinel is a pretty ubiquitous pocket knife in France and available in a variety of sizes. I particularly like this one because it reminds me of a particular scene from near the end of *Kelly's Heroes*. Tank commander Odd Ball (Donald Sutherland) is sitting back while his guys fix the Sherman, when Big Joe (Telly Savalas) asks him what he's doing, 'I'm drinking wine and eating cheese and catching some rays' is his relaxed answer. It's an Opinel knife that you need to cut the cheese on those equally relaxed 4x4 trips, regardless of whether you're driving a Sherman or a Land Rover.

Gerber from Portland are noted for the manufacture of multi-tools, but the company also makes folding knives such as this one. It's a Gerber 625 and has a rubberised handle with an asymmetric pattern and a single blade that locks open. It has a lovely action and is a quality piece of kit. It has a tiny Land Rover oval logo on one side of the blade.

This Herbertz lock knife's wooden handle and tooled brass ends remind me of the engraved pistols favoured by gunfighters, at least in the Hollywood interpretations of their stories. For many though, the famous Victorinox Swiss Army knife is the definitive pocket knife. It has important attributes and different knives have different and comprehensive selections of extra tools. This basic one has a corkscrew that is a quality item that gets a positive pull on a wine cork, while the bottle opener is also a useful tool.

# MULTI-TOOLS

Gerber started in 1939 making small orders of cutlery with the vision of Joseph R. Gerber pushing the company forward. The company, headquartered in Oregon, moved into the utility market during the 1950s and 1960s. It currently makes axes, handsaws, flashlights and digging tools. Gerber tools exude quality, as do other well-known brands such as Leatherman. Such tools have an array of tools that fold into the handle including a hacksaw blade, wire cutter, scissors, Philips screwdriver, pliers, wire strippers and a main blade.

The famous Swiss Army knives and multi-tools from the likes of Leatherman and Gerber are handy and convenient because they can be folded up and carried in a pocket or belt pouch.

The corkscrew tool incorporated into many Swiss Army knives is a quality item that gets a solid pull on the cork of a wine bottle, proving useful on 4x4 camping trips.

# SHARPENING STONE

Pocket knives can be sharpened on a medium- or fine-grain sharpening or whetstone stone with a few drops of oil spread on the surface. Hold the handle of the knife in one hand and place the blade across the stone. Press down with the fingers of the other hand and stroke the blade following a circular motion. After several strokes, reverse the blade and stroke the opposite side, following the same type of motion. Use a light, even pressure. A thin blade overheats quickly and can lose its temper. The wire edge or burr that may be left on a knife blade after whetting may be removed by stropping both sides on a soft wood block, canvas or leather. In field conditions, any smooth flat stone can be used to sharpen a knife with a drop of engine oil or saliva, but a whetstone will result in a sharper edge.

Knives are easily sharpened on an oilstone with a circular motion. An axe can be sharpened in the same way, but a heavily used axe head may need filing.

The concept of the axe goes back to the Stone Age, making it the longest-used cutting device in human history. Axes are essential for cutting and splitting wood, and a good hand axe is all that's needed to prepare wood for small campfires.

# BATTERY WELDING

Gather two batteries, two sets of jump leads and a welding rod, and it is possible to weld in a safe and timely manner. Wire the batteries in series to produce 24 volts of electric feed that, when earthed to bare metal, can be utilised as a primitive arc welder. You will need to carry a variety of welding rods and eye protection as well as an extra set of cables or a shortened thick-gauge cable to connect the batteries in a series.

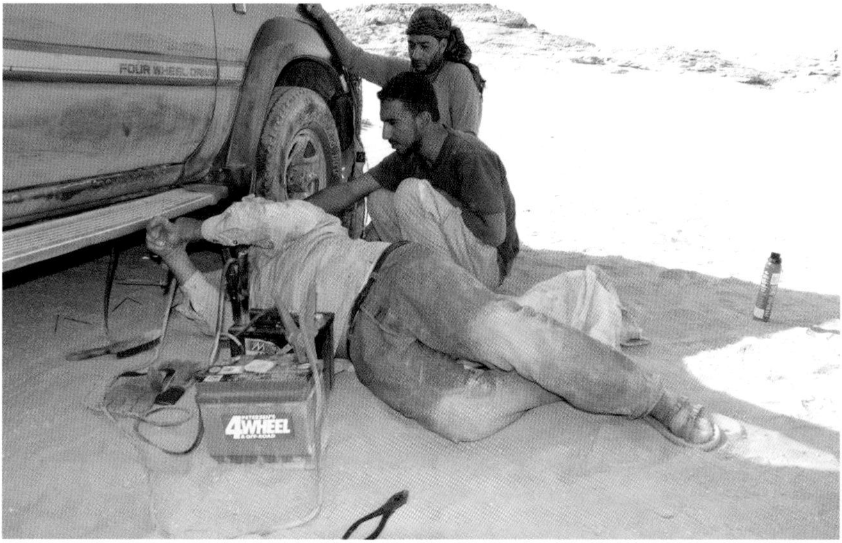

*Above*: Two batteries connected in series with jump leads give 24v that can be used with a welding rod and an earth to make weld repairs.

*Right*: Improvising a windbreak while adjusting the valves on a Willys Jeep in order to keep blowing sand out of the mechanical components.

A failed air intake hose repaired with duct tape and a disposable plastic water bottle.

Airing down in preparation for soft sand requires a primitive tool – in this case a rock – to push the tip of the valve in and a more sophisticated tool – a gauge – to measure the pressure.

One way to keep tools that are frequently needed to hand is to mount them outside the 4x4. A Bulldog shovel comes in handy for many tasks beyond digging out a stuck 4x4 including digging latrines and fire pits.

These plastic sand/mud ladders and shovel are carried on the side of this Land Rover's roof rack.

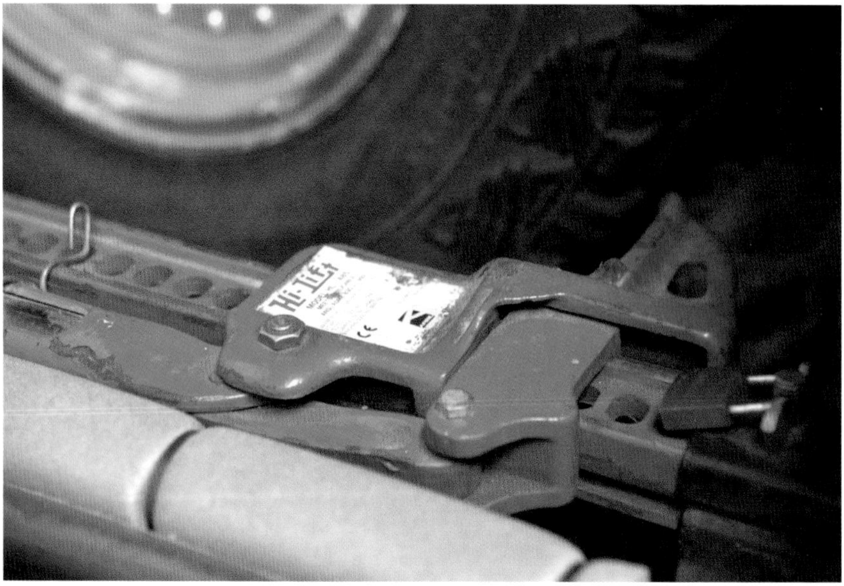


Hi-Lift jacks are heavy and cumbersome so should be secured to a vehicle being used off-road. This Jeep has mounts within its load bed.

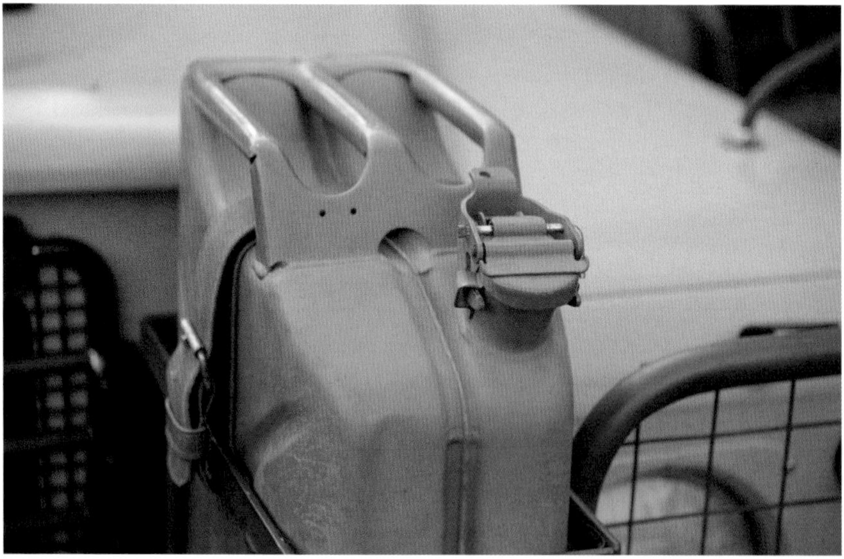

Jerrycans for additional fuel and water are heavy when full, so can be safely carried on racks on the outside or roof racks of a 4x4.

In arid conditions, dust can be a real problem in numerous ways so cameras and associated equipment should be carried in dustproof protective containers.

A vehicle's roof rack itself is a useful tool and enables a 4x4 to be used to carry significant loads, such as the pair of canoes on top of this Land Rover Series III 109in Station Wagon.

## FUEL FILTRATION

In remote places where 4x4s may require refuelling from jerrycans, it is worth filtering the fuel – petrol or diesel – that comes out of them to catch any flakes of paint or rust from inside the can. This prevents such flakes from causing blockages in fuel lines, fuel pumps and injectors or carburettors. In an emergency, an old t-shirt or women's tights can be used as a filter – the finer the weave, the better filter the fabric will be.

# FIRST AID

First aid is the emergency care a sick or injured person gets in the first instance. Often, it may be the only care someone needs, while it may help others until paramedics arrive or they are taken to the hospital. Learn the basic techniques for dealing with cuts, burns and blisters and learn cardiopulmonary resuscitation before going too far off the beaten track. Check for required vaccinations before travelling abroad.

Carry a first aid kit aboard your 4x4. This kit should include the necessities: scissors, adhesive, gauze, soap, a CPR mouth barrier and an emergency whistle. Small cuts and scrapes can quickly become infected if left untreated, so keep bandages and antiseptic on hand. Add bottles of sunscreen and insect repellent as well because sunburn and infected bug bites can end a trip overnight. Lip balm is useful, as wind, cold, sun, strenuous activity, not enough water, and elevation can all lead to your lips needing extra

## FIRST AID KIT ESSENTIALS

- Adhesive tape
- Antibacterial gel/wipes
- Antiseptic cream
- Bandages and gauze dressings
- Burn cream
- CPR mouth barrier
- Disposable gloves
- Emergency blanket and whistle
- Medication, including Piriteze/allergy pills and paracetamol/Tylenol
- Scissors and tweezers
- Snake bite kit (depending on destination)
- Soap
- Sticking plasters/band-aids

attention. Keep this handy and apply often. Wear sunglasses to protect your eyes from glare and improve your vision when driving on sand dunes by wearing sunglasses. Sunglasses, especially polarised ones, can highlight gradations or changes in the sand, helping you to easily pick out depressions or holes so you don't unexpectedly drive into them.

## DEHYDRATION

Dehydration can cause serious physical problems and make you more susceptible to other problems, such as frostbite and hypothermia. Because there is a large amount of fluid loss in hot and cold conditions, you should drink a minimum of four litres of water a day when undertaking heavy physical activity.

Water is usually available, either from streams or lakes or by melting snow or ice. A limiting factor for the latter may be the amount of fuel needed to melt snow or ice. Where possible, water should be obtained from running streams or lakes. The milky water from glacial streams must be allowed to stand until the sediment settles, and muddy river water should be filtered.

When running water is not available, ice or snow must be melted. The former produces more water in less time. When melting snow, first put a small amount into the cooking pot, then gradually add more as it melts. Continue this process until there is enough water for cooking and drinking. Use all available stoves as this is a time-consuming operation. Melting and boiling enough snow for a drink may take 30–40 minutes. The water should be purified by boiling vigorously for some minutes.

Ensure that as much of the daily intake as possible is hot drinks, such as soup and cocoa. Coffee and caffeinated tea are not dehydrating, although caffeine is a mild diuretic. This means that it causes your kidneys to flush extra sodium and water from the body through urine. A main meal should begin with soup, and between meal snacks should include a hot drink.

**Prevention:** the minimum daily liquid requirement for someone performing demanding physical work in the cold is 4 litres per day. By the time you feel thirsty, you are already dehydrated. Drink whenever possible, particularly during halts. Ensure that canteens are full before moving on. Check your urine spots; dark yellow or brown indicates dehydration. Red indicates a severe condition needing immediate medical evacuation.

**Symptoms:** lack of appetite; dry mouth, tongue and throat; stomach cramps and/or vomiting; headaches.

**Treatment:** keep the patient warm, give plenty of fluids and make them rest.

## HYPOTHERMIA

Hypothermia is a lowering of the temperature of the body's inner core. This happens when the body loses heat faster than it can produce it. You must be able to recognise the symptoms of hypothermia and treat it immediately.

**Prevention:** stay physically fit and keep active. Keep clothes dry. Eat properly and often, and drink plenty of liquids, at least 4 litres per day when performing physically demanding work. Be prepared for and know how to deal with quick changes in weather. Bivouac or camp early before judgement is clouded by fatigue.

**Symptoms:** shallow breathing or absence of breathing; faint or undetectable pulse; the patient is first cold then stops shivering; loss of feeling, poor coordination, and trouble walking; impaired speech; confusion; withdrawn appearance; depressed or down/upset; and/or uncoordinated. An uncaring attitude and/or glassy stare are also clues.

**Treatment:** prevent any further heat loss. Get the patient out of the wind and into the best shelter available. Replace any wet clothing with dry and place the patient in a sleeping bag, if one is available. Place as much insulation as possible between the patient and the ground. Add heat by the best available means to the victim's neck, groin and sides of chest. This can be done by using a hot water bottle, campfire, or your own body heat. Provide the patient with something warm and nutritious to drink if he/she is conscious. Calories may be added by using sugar in hot, sweet drinks. Do not massage the patient. Do not give alcohol to the patient. Evacuate the victim to the nearest medical treatment facility as soon as possible. This condition is life threatening until normal body temperature is restored.

## FROSTBITE

Frostbite results when tissues freeze from exposure to temperatures below 32 degrees Fahrenheit. The degree of injury depends upon the wind chill factor, length of exposure time and proper protection. Persons with a history of cold injury are prone to frostbite. There may be a tingling, stinging, an aching sensation, or a cramping pain. The skin first turns red and then becomes pale grey or waxy white. Frostbite can be classified as superficial or deep.

**Prevention:** frostbite is preventable if individuals take care of themselves. It seldom occurs in people who are maintaining enough

### TIPS TO HELP PREVENT FROSTBITE

- Do not wear tight boots and socks.
- Use the buddy system to check exposed areas, especially in windy conditions.
- Carry extra socks and mitten liners.
- Do not stay still for long periods.
- Use caution when cold and wind are combined.
- Check hands and feet during halts.
- Ensure you eat well and have hot drinks as often as possible.

body heat. It is commonly associated with an overall body heat loss resulting from poor equipment, reduced food intake, dehydration, fatigue, injury or a combination of these factors. The feet, hands, ears and exposed areas of the face are most easily hurt by frostbite and must receive constant care.

**Symptoms of superficial frostbite:** redness occurs, followed by powdery flaking of the skin. Affected areas of dark-skinned individuals may appear dull and greyish. Blister formation occurs 24 to 30 hours after exposure, followed by the flaking of superficial skin.

**Symptoms of deep frostbite:** loss of feeling occurs in the affected area, leaving it pale yellow and waxy looking. When the frostbitten area thaws, it is painful.

Frozen tissue may feel solid or wooden to the touch. When exposed to inside temperatures, blisters may appear in 12 to 36 hours. Discolouration (red-violet) appears 1 to 5 days after the injury. Gangrene can result.

**Treatment:** determine whether the frostbite is superficial or deep. If the exposure time was short, the frostbite will probably be superficial. If the exposure time was lengthy, the frostbite will probably be deep. Move the casualty to a warm and sheltered area. Do not rewarm the affected area by massaging or exposing it to open fire. Rewarm the face, nose, or ears by placing hands on the frozen area. Rewarm frostbitten hands by placing them under clothing and against the body. Close the clothing to prevent further loss of body heat. Rewarm the feet by removing boots and socks. Place the bare feet under the clothing and against the abdomen of a buddy. Once the feet are warmed put on dry socks and boots, if available. If the patient must wear the wet socks and boots, they should exercise their feet by wiggling their toes. Loosen tight clothing and remove jewellery. Improve circulation by exercise. Do not allow the patient to use alcohol or tobacco. Alcohol increases loss of body heat, and tobacco causes the narrowing of blood vessels in the arms and legs. Reassure the patient. Protect frozen tissue from further cold or trauma, and evacuate the casualty to the nearest medical treatment facility.

Deep frostbite is most common and harmful to the feet and less common to the hands and ears. When deep frostbite does occur, the victim should be moved to a sheltered area and evacuated to a medical treatment facility immediately. If possibly, do not allow the patient to walk if the feet are frozen and avoid treating or thawing the affected area. Thawing of deep frostbite in the field increases pain and invites infection, greater damage and gangrene. Do not try to thaw deep frostbite, let a medical professional do this.

## WIND CHILL

The combination of wind and low temperatures creates a condition known as wind chill. For example, with the wind calm and a temperature of -20 degrees Fahrenheit, there is little chance of wind chill. If the temperature is -20 degrees Fahrenheit and there is a wind of 20 knots, the equivalent chill temperature is -75 degrees Fahrenheit. Under these conditions there is great danger, and your exposed skin can freeze within 30 seconds. You can also create your own wind when you walk, run or ski.

## CARBON MONOXIDE POISONING

Carbon monoxide is a deadly odourless gas. Whenever a stove, fire, gasoline heater or internal combustion engine is used indoors, there is a danger of carbon monoxide poisoning. Fresh air in living and working environments is vital.

**Prevention:** use stoves and lanterns in well-ventilated areas and tents. Ensure that stoves and lanterns are functioning properly. Do not let people warm themselves by using engine exhausts. Always have windows open slightly in vehicles with a heater in use. Shut stoves off when sleeping.

**Symptoms:** headache, dizziness, confusion, yawning, weariness, nausea and ringing in the ears. Bright red colour on lips and skin. Victims may become drowsy and collapse suddenly.

**Treatment:** move the victim to open air. Keep the victim still and warm. If the victim is not breathing, administer mouth-to-mouth resuscitation. Administer cardiopulmonary resuscitation, if necessary. Immediately evacuate the victim to the nearest medical treatment facility.

## SNOW BLINDNESS

Snow blindness is caused by ultraviolet and ultra-blue rays of the sun being reflected from a snow-covered surface into the eyes. This condition can occur even in cloudy weather.

**Prevention:** wear sunglasses. If sunglasses are not available, make slitted glasses from cardboard, thin wood, tree bark or similar materials.

**Symptoms:** a scratchy sandy feeling under the eyelids; redness and watering of the eyes; a headache.

**Treatment:** blindfold the patient using a dark cloth. Reassure the patient and evacuate the patient to a medical treatment facility as soon as possible.

## SUNBURN

Sunburn is a serious hazard in desert conditions but also in snow because of the reflective qualities of snow, especially at higher elevations.

**Prevention:** use sunscreen and lip balm.

**Symptoms:** redness of skin with slight swelling. Prolonged exposure to the sun may cause pain and blistering and, in severe cases, chills, fever and headaches.

**Treatment:** soothing aftersun skin creams or aloe vera may be helpful if the swelling is not severe.

## TENT EYE

'Tent Eye' is an inflammation of the eye caused by fumes from stoves and lanterns used in poorly ventilated tents or shelters. It is prevented by proper ventilation of tents or shelters. The treatment is fresh air.

## TRENCH FOOT/IMMERSION FOOT

Trench foot and immersion foot are injuries caused by the prolonged exposure of the skin to cold or wet conditions, such as those found in jungles and rainforests. In extreme cases, the skin dies and amputation of the foot or leg may be necessary.

**Prevention:** change to dry socks at least daily. Dry and massage feet regularly and use foot powder. Dry boots at every opportunity.

**Symptoms:** in the early stages, the feet and toes are cold, numb and still, and walking becomes challenging. The feet swell and become painful.

**Treatment:** in the early stages keep the feet dry, clean and exposed to the air, but, in later stages, evacuate the victim to a medical treatment facility as soon as possible.

## CONSTIPATION

In very cold temperatures, people tend to put off the natural urge to have a bowel movement, resulting in constipation. This can be painful.

**Prevention:** eat fresh/peeled or canned fruits and eat regularly and remember to wash your hands often. Drink plenty of liquids. Try to have a daily bowel movement.

**Symptoms:** stomach cramps, dizziness and headaches.

**Treatment:** prevention is the best treatment. If symptoms persist, get medical help. In the meantime, drink lots of water and up your fibre intake.

## DIARRHOEA

Diarrhoea, loose, watery and possibly more-frequent bowel movements, is a common problem. It may be present alone or be associated with other symptoms, such as nausea, vomiting or abdominal pain. Luckily, it is usually short-lived, lasting no more than a few days. However, it can lead to dehydration.

**Prevention:** diarrhoea commonly affects people who travel to countries where there's inadequate sanitation and contaminated food. To reduce your risk, watch what you eat. Eat hot, well-cooked foods. Avoid raw fruits and vegetables unless you can peel them yourself. Also avoid raw or undercooked meats and dairy foods.

Watch what you drink. Drink bottled water, soda, beer or wine served in its original container. Avoid tap water and ice cubes. Use bottled water even for brushing your teeth. Keep your mouth closed while you shower. Drinks made with boiled water, such as coffee and tea, are probably safe. Remember that alcohol and caffeine can aggravate diarrhoea and worsen dehydration.

**Symptoms:** abdominal cramps or pain; bloating; nausea; vomiting; fever; urgent need to have a bowel movement.

**Treatment:** most cases of acute diarrhoea clear on their own within a couple of days without treatment. Antibiotics or anti-parasitic medications might help treat diarrhoea caused by bacteria or parasites. If a virus is causing your diarrhoea, antibiotics won't help. Replace the fluids and salts by drinking water with electrolytes, juice or broth. If drinking liquids upsets your stomach or causes vomiting, a doctor might recommend IV fluids. Water is a good way to replace fluids but doesn't contain the salts and electrolytes, minerals such as sodium and potassium that are essential for your body to function. Maintain your electrolyte levels by drinking fruit juice or eating soups.

## HEAT CRAMPS

Heat cramps are caused by an excessive loss of salt in the body. This loss of salt causes muscles to spasm, and they are unable to relax. After prolonged physical activity in a cold or wet environment, the signs and symptoms of heat cramps could appear in the arms, legs and/or stomach. It is possible to experience heat cramps in a cold-weather environment when undergoing extreme physical exertion.

**Symptoms:** muscle cramps in the arms, legs and/or stomach. The patient is pale, has wet skin and experiences dizziness and extreme thirst.

**Treatment:** drink plenty of water. Give the victim one canteen of water with one packet of salt stirred in. Have them drink the canteen of salted water over a 30-minute period. If the cramping of muscles continues, evacuate the patient to the nearest medical treatment facility as soon as possible.

## HEAT EXHAUSTION

Heat exhaustion is caused by dehydration and the loss of body salt from extreme physical activity in a hot-humid environment. It is also possible to experience heat exhaustion in a cold-weather environment when undergoing extreme physical exertion.

**Symptoms:** feeling dizzy, weak, and/or faint. The skin feels cool and moist to the touch. The patient may also feel nauseous and have a headache.

**Treatment:** drink liberal amounts of water to relieve the symptoms.

# ALTITUDE SICKNESS

Altitude sickness/acute mountain sickness (AMS) can occur if you travel to a high altitude too quickly. Breathing becomes difficult because it is not possible to take in as much oxygen. It can become a medical emergency if ignored. Symptoms of altitude sickness usually develop between 6 and 24 hours after reaching altitudes more than 2,500m above sea level. Altitude sickness does not only affect mountain climbers. Tourists travelling to cities that are 2,500m above sea level or higher, such as La Paz in Bolivia or Bogotá in Colombia, can also get altitude sickness. It is not possible to get altitude sickness in the UK because the highest mountain, Ben Nevis in Scotland, is only 1,345m above sea level.

If the symptoms of altitude sickness are ignored, they can lead to life-threatening conditions affecting the brain or lungs, such as High-Altitude Cerebral Oedema (HACE), a swelling of the brain caused by a lack of oxygen, and High-Altitude Pulmonary Oedema (HAPE), a build-up of fluid in the lungs. Both can be fatal.

**Symptoms:** headache; feeling and/or being sick; dizziness and/or tiredness; loss of appetite; shortness of breath.

**Prevention:** travel to altitudes above 2,500m slowly. Avoid flying directly to areas of high altitude. If possible, take 2–3 days to get used to high altitudes before going above 2,500m. Make sure you're drinking enough water. Avoid smoking and alcohol. Avoid strenuous exercise for the first 24 hours. Eat light but high-calorie foods.

**Treatment:** stop and rest where you are, and do not go any higher for at least 24 to 48 hours. If you have a headache, take ibuprofen or paracetamol. Make sure you're drinking enough water. Do not smoke or drink alcohol. If you do not feel any better after 24 hours, descend at least 500m.

When on 4x4 trips to hot places, it is not just the vehicle's fluid levels that need to be checked daily.

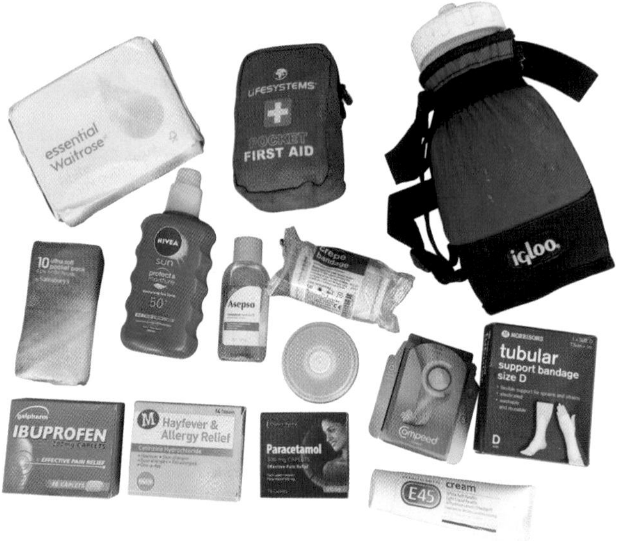


A basic first aid kit and associated things such as sun cream and toilet paper should be carried in a 4x4 in a place where the entire group knows where it is in case of emergency.

Water should be consumed frequently in order to avoid dehydration and heat exhaustion in arid climates or places where there is no shade.

Snow and ice can be melted to provide drinking water but is a time-consuming operation, so ample time to do this should be scheduled.

Disposable water bottles are falling out of favour for environmental reasons, but, in many places, they are still the only source of safe drinking water.

Where possible, water jerrycans should be filled to ensure an ample supply. Such jerrycans can be carried in special vehicle brackets.

There is a huge variety of drinking water bottles available, but these desert water bags are interesting. They were designed to keep water cool in hot conditions as they could be filled with water and hung on the outside of the vehicle. The movement caused seepage to evaporate and the contents to cool in the same way as cowboys' leather bota bags.

# GLOSSARY

| | |
|---|---|
| All-wheel drive | An all-wheel-drive vehicle has a powertrain capable of providing power to all its wheels. |
| Anchor point | A point by which something is held securely or fastened; also called recovery point |
| Basha sheet | A waterproof canvas or plastic sheet with eyelets or loops on the perimeter |
| Bivouac/Bivvy | A temporary camp without tents |
| Bota bag | A soft leather canteen designed to carry water in the great outdoors |
| Bow shackle | A bow shaped metal loop which is closed by a threaded pin |
| Cable | The wire rope used on winches |
| Camel Trophy | An international 4x4 vehicle-oriented competition held annually between 1980 and 1998 |
| CJ | Civilian Jeep |
| Compass | A device that shows the cardinal directions used for navigation and geographic orientation |
| Differential | A gear train with three drive shafts required to get drive to wheels on an axle |

| | |
|---|---|
| D-shackle | A U-shaped metal loop with a straight pin closure, making a D shape |
| Fairlead | A device to guide a winch cable onto a winch drum |
| Glamping | A hybrid of 'glamorous' and 'camping' that describes a luxury style of camping with amenities |
| Lifting eye | Used on 4x4x and other equipment to facilitate their movement when being recovered; also called a towing eye |
| Mechanical advantage | The force amplification achieved by using a tool, mechanical device or machine system. |
| Pocket knife | A foldable knife with one or more blades that fold into the handle, also known as a jackknife or penknife |
| PTO | Power take off, commonly a drive shaft installed on a 4x4 enabling a winch to be powered by the engine |
| Recovery strap | Used to 'recover' a stuck 4x4 vehicle by towing; also called a tow strap |
| Roof tent | A tent fitted to the roof or bed of a 4x4 that enables users to sleep above the vehicle |
| Sand mats | Also known as traction mats, they are used to offer traction in difficult terrain such as sand, snow and soft ground |
| Satnav | Navigation system dependent on information received from satellites |
| Snatch blocks | A pulley in a metal casing through which a winch line is routed |

| | |
|---|---|
| Splice | Forms a joint between two ropes or two parts of the same rope by partly untwisting and then interweaving their strands |
| Synthetic rope | Constructed by braiding different synthetic materials together to create a finished winch rope |
| Topography | The arrangement of natural and man-made physical features of an area |
| Torque | A rotating force produced by an engine's crankshaft. The more torque an engine produces, the greater its ability to perform work measured in Newton-metres (Nm) or foot-pounds (ft/lb) |
| Towing hitch | A device attached to the chassis of a vehicle for towing a trailer |
| Transfer box/case | A part of the drivetrain of 4x4 vehicles that transfers power from the transmission to the front and rear axles by means of drive shafts and may contain low range gears for off-road use |
| Tree strop | A name for straps used as lifting straps, anchor straps for pulling that include reinforced eyes |
| Wading depth | The maximum depth of water a 4x4 can cross |
| Wheelbase | The horizontal distance between the centres of the front and rear wheels |

# FURTHER READING


Cranfield, Ingrid & Harrington Richard, *Off the Beaten track*, Wexas International Ltd (1977)

Dimbleby, Nick, *Camel Trophy: The Definitive History*, Porter Press International (2021)

Drake, Peter G., *The Complete Practical Guide to Camping, Hiking & Wilderness Skills*, Hermes House (2004)

Fry, Eric C., *The Shell Book of Knots and Ropework*, Alden Press (1977)

Fuchs, Vivian & Hillary, Edmund, *The Crossing of Antarctica*, Penguin Books (1958)

Land Rover Ltd, *Land Rover's Manual for Africa*, Land Rover Ltd (1989)

Land Rover Ltd, *Winching in Safety*, The Land Rover Directory (1989)

Mears, Ray, *Bushcraft*, Hodder and Stoughton (2002)

Outward Bound, *Map and Compass Handbook*, Ward Lock (1994)

Philpott, Don, *Britain Goes Camping*, National Trust Books (2011)

Pritchard-Jones, Sian & Gibbons, Bob, *Africa Overland*, Bradt Travel Guides Ltd (1991)

Ryan, Chris, *Chris Ryan's Ultimate Survival Guide*, Century (2003)

Slessor, Tim, *First Overland*, George G. Harrap & Co Ltd (1957)

Thurkettle, Vincent, *The Wood Fire Handbook*, Octopus Publishing Group Ltd (2012)

If you have the right equipment, the weather should not impact your trips too much. It is said that 'there is no such thing a bad weather, just the wrong clothing'.

# LIST OF ADVENTURES

Since the earliest days of motoring, and before the advent of the 4x4, there have been significant overland journeys made in vehicles. Following the epic race from Peking to Paris in 1908, several trans-continental journeys were made, including the Court Treatt Expedition, which was the first to drive a motor vehicle from Cape Town, South Africa to Cairo, Egypt. The party of six people, led by Major Chaplin Court Treatt and his wife Stella Maud Court Treatt (née Hinds), set off in two strengthened Crossley 25/30 light trucks with tender-type bodies in September 1924 and reached Cairo 16 months later in January 1926, having covered 12,732 miles.

The Croisière Noire was a French expedition that crossed the African continent from north to south between October 1924 and June 1925. It was organised by André Citroën in order to promote his brand of vehicles. The Croisière Jaune was a subsequent French trans-Asian expedition of 1931–32. It was also organised by Citroën in order to promote its P17 Kégresse half-track vehicles. The expedition started in Beirut and, in early 1932, reached the East China Sea. These expeditions paved the way for many more, made for a variety of reasons including surveying for road and air routes, exploration purposes and for the challenge of being the first to make certain journeys. It wasn't until much later that the idea of recreational overland travel took off in the aftermath of World War Two, with epic journeys including Ben Carlin's circumnavigation of the world in a Ford GPA, an amphibious version of the Willys Jeep.

# EUROPE

If you are planning a 4x4 adventure in Europe, it is worth remembering that although some places do not have much in the way of dirt roads, Europe does offer some remote hidden gems to visit. Europe is heavily populated and has more surfaced road per square kilometre than any other continent, plus much of its wilderness is in national parks where off-road driving is prohibited. Despite this, there is still plenty of wilderness to explore, you just need to know where to go.

**The Alps:** The Alps are the highest and most extensive mountain range in Europe, running for 1,200km (750 miles) through Switzerland, France, Monaco, Italy, Germany, Austria, Liechtenstein and Slovenia. The highest mountain in the range is Mont Blanc – this dominant peak reaches 4,810m (15,781 ft). Tracks and minor roads follow in the footsteps of adventurers, mountaineers and even Hannibal and Napoleon who crossed these mountain passes on foot and horseback.

**Iceland:** You need a ferry to get to Iceland from Europe, but it is worth the effort as it provides some of the best European off-road adventures. Much of the volcanic country is wild and there are beautiful landscapes to see. Iceland has a lot of 4×4 tours available and hiring a 4x4 after arriving is a popular and easy way to visit. The high mountain tracks open in the summer and gravel roads cross the lava and ash deserts in Iceland's mountainous interior and enable visits to glaciers and thermal pools.

**Ireland:** The Wild Atlantic Way, 2,600km (1,600 miles) in length, is one of the longest coastal routes in the world. Taking in the remote minor roads along the entire west coast of Ireland, it winds its way from the Inishowen Peninsula in the north to the picturesque town of Kinsale, County Cork, in the south, passing through the counties of Clare, Galway, Kerry, Leitrim, Mayo and Sligo. It is a coastal route that lives up to the hype, as around most corners of this route, will be magnificent views of the west coast's rugged shoreline.

**Portugal:** Portugal is one of the best countries in Europe in which to explore a huge network of dirt tracks, making it a top destination for 4x4 travellers. Wild camping is not permitted in Portugal, so there are numerous rural accommodation options, including registered campsites and B&Bs.

**Pyrenees:** The Spanish Pyrenees are the least visited part of the dramatic mountains straddling the border between France and Spain. The entire region is beautiful, comprising forested foothills, secret valleys and soaring snow-capped mountains, it is some of the best mountain driving in Europe. Forest tracks offer challenging driving on the steep climbs and the old smugglers' trails that cross the border offer tight hairpin bends.

**Romania:** Bordered by Bulgaria, Hungary, Moldova, Serbia and Ukraine, Romania is the 12th largest country in Europe. Its terrain is divided between mountains, hills and plains so there is plenty of choice of 4x4 tracks and wild camping opportunities. This region includes the Carpathian Mountains, which are split between three major ranges: Eastern (Oriental), Southern (the Transylvanian Alps) and Western Carpathians.

**Scotland:** Scotland may be short on dirt roads but has all the other essential ingredients for the 4x4 trip, including beautiful mountain scenery and welcoming towns and villages. Touring Scotland in a 4x4 is easy and trips can be short or long but don't miss the rugged beauty of the west coast or the dramatic mountains of Glen Coe.

## AUSTRALIA

In many ways Australia's great outdoors is a 4x4 paradise because of its size and history that led to the establishment of numerous routes through the outback, which can still be driven in a 4x4. A selection includes the following:

**Binns Track:** The Binns Track is an epic 4x4 adventure that passes through spectacular scenery and explores some of the lesser-known parts of Northern Territory.

**Birdsville Track:** This was established as a cattle route and comprises two tracks to make up the famed Birdsville Track. The Inside Track follows the original stock path, while the Outside Track – created by travellers as a safer route – avoids the Diamantina floodplain. The popular route is primarily a stony track with large pebbles and sand.

**Canning Stock Route:** This is renowned as one of the toughest and remotest 4x4 routes in the world. It passes through the vast deserts of Western Australia. It runs to Halls Creek in the Kimberley region from Wiluna in the mid-west, a total distance of around 1,850km (1,150 miles), making it the longest historic stock route in the world.

**Cape York Track:** The old telegraph track, used in the 1880s to connect Cairns with Thursday Island, is a rough road accessible only during Australia's dry season. It is located on Cape York, in tropical north Queensland, and while it is only 350km (217 miles) long, it requires a 4x4. The track is generally narrow, with some sections being very rocky and eroded as it follows the original telegraph line on the Cape York peninsula.

**Gibb River Road:** This route passes through the heart of the Kimberley region of Western Australia from Derby to Wyndham. Much of the Gibb River Road is corrugated track and, owing to the popularity of this scenic 4x4 route, it can be busy from May to September. Stretching 660km (410 miles), Gibb River Road is noted as a fantastic trip for 4x4 drivers regardless of experience.

**Gunbarrel Highway:** This is an isolated desert track in Northern Territory, South Australia and Western Australia. It consists of about 1,350km (840 miles) of off-road terrain and connects Victory Downs in Northern Territory to Carnegie Station in Western Australia. Parts of the track are only suitable for high clearance 4x4 vehicles and should only be attempted by confident drivers.

**The Nullarbor:** A tour of the Nullarbor offers an unforgettable 4x4 adventure, and the ideal challenge for 4WD beginners. Covering more than 1,250km (770 miles) from South Australia's Eyre Peninsula to the Western Australian goldfields, the Nullarbor combines virtually barren, treeless plains with the spectacular ocean sights of the Great Australian Bight. Its remoteness means that carrying additional water and fuel supplies is essential.

**Red Centre Way:** This offers a classic 4x4 adventure along an 1,140km (708 mile) loop beginning and ending in Alice Springs, Northern Territory.

## US

**California:** The original Jeepers Jamboree is arguably the beginning of organised, recreational off-roading. It takes place on the Rubicon Trail from the foothills town of Georgetown over the Sierra Nevada mountain range, and started in 1952. The route is unchanged: vehicles still head east on approximately 45 miles of paved road to Loon Lake where it's time to engage 4x4, air down the tyres and start the gruelling 17 miles of off-roading, with an overnight camp en route. The now numerous Jeep-sanctioned Jeep Jamborees are off-road adventure weekends for Jeep owners and organised all over the US.

**Utah:** Almost as famous is the Easter Jeep Safari, an annual event where four-wheelers come to drive trails through the rough terrain, and so-called slick rock, of the backcountry in the Moab, Utah, area. The Jeep Safari was started in 1967. Over the years, it has increased to become the nine-day event it is now. Big Saturday, on the Saturday of Easter weekend, remains the culmination of the event. It now also holds a Labour Day Camp Out and other club outings, as well as working to keep the Moab trails open.